TICKETS OF THE
WEST MIDLANDS PTE
PART 4
1983 – 1986

ROBIN OLIVER

The Transport Ticket Society
2000

Cover photograph:
WMPTE bus 4613 (JOV613P), Daimler Fleetline with Park
Royal body at Midland Bus Musuem, Wythall, 28 June 1990.
[Robin Oliver]

Comments etc. regarding this publication are welcome;
please write to the Society's Publications Officer:

David Harman
24 Frankfield Rise
Tunbridge Wells
TN2 5LF

E-Mail: David.Harman@btinternet.com

© Copyright Robin Oliver, 2000

ISBN 0 903209 39 X

Published by
The Transport Ticket Society
81 Pilgrims Way, Kemsing, Sevenoaks, TN15 6TD

Printed by
Paterson Printing Ltd.
Tunbridge Wells

Index

Introduction

First of all, may I offer my thanks to all those who kindly purchased copies of "*Tickets of the West Midlands PTE 1969-1983.*"

It has to be said that the subject scarcely lends itself to thrills, excitement or levity, so perhaps these three volumes were not really suitable for light entertainment or bedtime reading! However, I hope that collectors of transport tickets found them useful and informative works of reference, to dip into as required.

There must inevitably have been some mistakes, so I'm surprised that there was so little feedback from readers. A few errors have come to light - some of them caused by misprints which escaped correction - and a small amount of additional information has turned up. Corrections and extra details are given in Appendix G of this publication, together with a substantial number of additional illustrations relating to tickets described in the original volumes.

I would especially like to thank the PSV Circle and the Omnibus Society for their generous reviews, and also the former WMPTE for kindly publishing details of the publications in their staff newspaper, "Fare."

When the original volumes "went to press" in 1983, it was known that the Government was planning a "shake-up" of the PTEs, but exactly what was in the wind was far from certain. Many enthusiasts no doubt hoped that bus services would be handed back to the erstwhile municipal operators, with perhaps some new ones appearing. Perhaps some of us tried to imagine a Metrobus in Walsall Corporation blue, or a Leyland National in Wolverhampton green and yellow! What sort of livery might Dudley or Solihull decide to adopt, if they became bus operators for the first time? Actually, in 1996, a Metrobus *was* painted in Walsall blue - and very attractive it looked. Only one thing was certain, back in 1983: for better or worse (depending on one's viewpoint) the Government was committed to the abolition of the PTEs' "political masters," namely the Metropolitan County Councils, of which West Midlands was one. This took place on the scheduled date, 1st April 1986.

In the meantime, the reorganisation plans for the bus operating industry were announced, and it became clear that all sections of the industry would be involved, not just the PTEs. Sadly, there would be no return to municipal bus fleets. The reshaping plan was set out in the bitterly-opposed Transport Act 1985, and became known as the "Deregulation" policy. Many long established rules and regulations affecting bus operation - often dating back to the famous Road Traffic Act of 1930 - would be abolished, particularly the "protectionist" legislation which had largely prevented competition between operators.

Putting it very simply, the purpose of Deregulation was twofold:-
1) To allow and encourage new or existing bus operators to compete with each other, in the same way as any other business.
2) By means of the above, to reduce the amount of public money being paid out to subsidise uneconomic services. Limited subsidies would still be available for those routes or journeys which were socially desirable but not commercially viable.

WMPTE were required, as part of the Deregulation legislation, to transfer their buses and operating staff to a new limited company which (initially) would be wholly-owned by the seven District Councils of the West Midlands County - namely Birmingham, Coventry, Dudley, Sandwell, Solihull, Walsall and Wolverhampton. (Although the WM County Council was duly abolished on 1st April 1986, the county itself remained in existence.) It was likely that the new bus company would eventually be privatised, which is, of course, what happened. Deregulation Day was set for Sunday 26th October 1986, and

on the previous day WMPTE ceased to be a bus operator after just over 17 years. However, the PTE remained in existence as a non-operating organisation, to perform certain remaining functions. They would:
1) Liaise with British Rail with regard to the provision of local train services in the WM County.
2) Monitor all bus services in the County, irrespective of operator.
3) Deal with the tenders and subsidies relating to uneconomic services or journeys.
4) Issue pensioners / disabled passes, and (although it took some years to achieve) issue general passes which would be valid on all bus operators' services in the County.
5) Look after bus stations, shelters etc.
6) Provide a telephone "hotline" for timetable enquiries.

Since 1990, the PTE (in its post-Deregulation role) has been known as Centro.

And so, on 26th October 1986, a "brand new" company, known as West Midlands Travel Ltd., took over the familiar blue and cream buses of the West Midlands. Of course, to most people, it wasn't really a new operator at all. Merely the same old "Wumpty" with a new name and logo. A modified livery was introduced, using the lighter shade of blue which WMPTE had employed on Metrobuses, but this was only the first of numerous livery styles revolving around blue, cream, silver and grey, relieved by red stripes. In 1996, the company (by then owned by National Express Ltd.) changed its fleet name to Travel West Midlands, accompanied by a new logo.

Obviously, the story of WMT/TWM tickets (and the separate range of Centro tickets) must wait until the future.

This publication records the story of WMPTE tickets from 1st April 1983 to 25th October 1986 - a short period, but a lot of ground to cover!

As before, I have included a chronology of events, a Collectors Checklist, and (most important of all) plenty of illustrations.

I have also put my neck on the block and attempted to unravel the complicated history of WMPTE Scholars and Pensioners' passes going back as near to 1969 as I can. I don't pretend that these chapters tell the full story, but at least they scratch the surface of what was, hitherto, almost uncharted territory. I am grateful to Andrew Rysztogi for kindly providing numerous illustrations of Scholars Tickets, plus other details on the subject, and also Janet Asbury of Wolverhampton Education Dept., and Alan Walker.

My thanks go to the following for providing information or assistance in one way or another: Bob Davis, Mark Gauden, Don Jones, Colin Page, Peter Shelley, WMPTE, Control Systems Ltd., and (as always) to the PSV Circle, Omnibus Society and Ian Allan Ltd. for the valuable data obtained from their publications. Useful snippets came from all sorts of people and places, so I apologise if I have omitted anybody!

I am very grateful to Richard Rosa and David Harman for typing the manuscript onto computer and processing the illustrations.

Finally, I would like to offer a special word of thanks to Glynn Waite and Mike Lister of The Transport Ticket Society for the very hard work which they and their helpers put in to produce the three original volumes of "*Tickets of the West Midlands PTE.*"

I hope that you will find this sequel both interesting and useful.

Robin Oliver
Wolverhampton
July 2000

2

First of all, a brief outline of "the story so far ...."

The 1970's was a fascinating period for those interested in WMPTE tickets, with such a wide variety of different types in use, but in 1970 the PTE had decided that the newly introduced Bell Punch Autofare system (designed purely for one-man-operation) (Fig 1) was the type best suited to their future requirements, and a conversion programme was set in motion.

Fig 1 - Autofare 1

Gradually, all other types were phased out, yet surprisingly it took as long as 10 years to achieve total standardisation on Autofare (or Autofare 1, as it later became known), during which time the takeover of a large slice of Midland Red (in 1973) and Coventry City Transport (1974) added several hundred Setright Speed machines to the PTE's collection.

Also, one or two short-lived fare collection systems made a fairly brief appearance in the 1970's: some Sabloc Farestat machines in Wolverhampton and a single Videmat in West Bromwich.

Sadly, all variety came to an end on 13th December 1980, when the last Ultimate machines were retired from service in Wolverhampton District, and crew operation ceased. From the following day Autofare 1 reigned supreme, and only one type of ticket - the Set A7 version (Fig 2) - could be found anywhere in the PTE's vast and far-flung territory.

Fig 2 - Autofare 1

T.I.M. and Setright machines had also survived into 1980, but had been phased out a short time earlier.

The supremacy of Autofare 1 was destined to last less than 18 months, because in May 1982 a new type of bus (the MCW Metrobus Mk II) ushered in a new type of ticket machine - the computerised Autofare 3. All buses of this type received Autofare 3 sets from new. No Metrobus Mk IIs ever ran with Autofare 1 machines.

A brief description of Autofare 3 was given in *Part 1*, but a fuller write-up can be found in Appendix B, later in this volume.

In the Autumn of 1982 brief trials were conducted with a brace of TimTronic machines fitted to buses working from Birmingham's Cotteridge Garage. Some rather neat titled rolls were used, with the "WM" symbol in blue, but the experiment was short lived.

On 12th January 1983, the WM County Council Passenger Transport Committee agreed to finance the replacement of all Autofare 1 machines with other types, and a large order for Autofare 3 sets was authorised. It was not certain at this stage whether the entire fleet would be converted to this system. The PTE wanted to keep their options open, so that

they could take advantage of any new developments in fare collection technology that might come along.

Autofare 3

On 1st April 1983, the situation was that just over 200 buses (all Metrobus Mk IIs) were equipped with Autofare 3, and the remainder of the fleet had Autofare 1 - with the exception of 20 non-PSV minibuses which had no fare collection equipment, and open-topper 3867 which had only a farebox.

Conversion of the fleet to the new system was loosely expected to be completed between July 1983 and the Autumn of 1984, but things did not work out like that.

In fact the first conversions took place somewhat earlier than anticipated (June, or possibly late May) but a small number of Autofare 1 sets lasted right through until October 1986. The last ones were probably replaced immediately before Deregulation and none (as far as I know) were used by West Midlands Travel Ltd. Generally speaking, Autofare 1 machines were retained on buses with a short life expectancy, but a few of the more modern vehicles (such as Fleetlines 6621 and 6628, latterly based in Wolverhampton) somehow slipped through the net. (6628, incidentally, had been one of the TimTronic buses in 1982.)

As a general guide, the Metrobus Mk Is were converted to Autofare 3 first (mostly by the end of 1983), followed by the Leyland Nationals and then other types. The ex-B.M.M.O. Nationals were initially excluded from the scheme, but by 1985 some had received new machines.

The same style of Autofare 3 ticket (Set A10) remained in use until 1985 (Fig 3), but a surprising number of colour shade and printing variations could be found. Advertisements first appeared on the backs in April 1984, and for the interest of readers I have included an illustrated appendix of these. (Appendix D.)

Fig 3 - Autofare 3

In June 1985, tickets appeared on noticeably thinner paper than previously. These are shown in the Checklist as Set A12, and they gradually replaced the A10 type. The design was identical.

One of the problems with Autofare 3 was the costly wastage of partly used rolls, caused by the practice of replacing them with new rolls to avoid the bus running out of tickets whilst in service. The obvious answer was to rejoin the remnants together to make complete rolls, but there was no convenient way of doing it.

The PTE's staff newspaper "*Fare*" (July 1984) reported that two Birmingham inspectors, Jim Evans and Kevin O'Reilly, had designed a re-rolling machine for this purpose. Their first machine was hand operated, but they later produced a motorised version which was successfully employed at Harborne Garage. The report went on to say that the PTE were interested in acquiring a more robust version suitable for intensive usage, but no subsequent details are known. A spokesman claimed that if each garage re-rolled only 5 ticket rolls a week, it could save £25,000 a year.

Off Peak Fares

On 2nd October 1983, a system of reduced off peak fares was introduced, whereby 32p (which was then the normal fare for 4 or 5 stages) became the maximum fare payable for any number of additional stages. For people making long journeys this meant a very substantial reduction, but there was no benefit for those travelling 5 stages or less. The 32p maximum fare (16p for children) applied at the following times:

Monday - Friday: 9.30 - 3.30, 6.00 - 11.29.
Weekends and Bank Holiday Mondays: All day up to 11.29.

The scheme (which became known as MaxiFare) was basically restricted to the WM County, but was also extended to Wombourne (a village in Staffordshire, just outside Wolverhampton). Generally speaking, a different fare structure applied to journeys starting or finishing outside the WM County.

Because of its length, route 159 (Birmingham to Coventry) was split into two zones, with a maximum off peak fare of 64p for the full journey. Understandably, they felt that 32p for a journey of nearly 20 miles, was pushing generosity a bit too far!

Limited Stop route 900 (Halesowen - Birmingham - Coventry) introduced in May 1985 and replacing the 159 on Mondays to Saturdays, had 3 fare zones, with a maximum fare of 96p.

As mentioned later, the prices of Daytripper tickets and Off Peak Travelcards were also reduced on 2nd October 1983.

Likewise, off peak rail fares within the WM County also came down. It meant that the price of a 2nd class return was only slightly higher than a single. On B.R., the time limit was extended to 11.59 p.m.

On 1st April 1985 there was a general fare increase, with 32p becoming 35p in the peak, but reverting to 32p off peak - just to complicate matters for all concerned! This did at least mean that passengers travelling 4 or 5 stages received an off-peak concession of 3p! No doubt they were overwhelmed with gratitude for this!

The PTE commissioned M. R. Harris, a lecturer in the Transport Studies Group at Aston University, to conduct a study into the effects and results of the off-peak fare scheme. His report, presented to the Passenger Transport Committee of the County Council on 9th January 1985, concluded that the scheme was basically successful and beneficial, but stated that losses to local rail services were "not insignificant" and also pointed out that only a small proportion of travellers were "able to take advantage of the opportunities offered." The report suggested that the off-peak maximum fare should perhaps be reduced to 3 stages instead of 4, or alternatively they could introduce a graduated off-peak fare structure. However, these suggestions were never implemented.

Subsequent fare increases were made, but the MaxiFare scheme continued basically unchanged until Deregulation, and was perpetuated by West Midlands Travel Ltd.

Guided Busway tickets
On 9th October 1984 WMPTE opened their famous (but rather short-lived) "guided busway" in Streetly Road, Short Heath, Birmingham. A lot was written about this at the time, but, basically, the central reservation in Streetly Road (used by the trams until July 1953) was concreted over and fitted with guide rails, which buses ran between. A batch of 14 Metrobus double deckers (8101-8114), painted in a special livery of silver, black and red, were fitted with small horizontal guide wheels attached to their front axles, in front of their conventional road wheels. When the bus entered the 600 metre "guided" section, these guide wheels would make contact with the rails and steer the vehicle automatically without the driver's aid. Rather like a reserved track tramway, but using buses which could run normally on ordinary roads. One critic claimed that the busway was really intended to be a launching ramp for Cruise missiles!

The route concerned was the 65 (Birmingham City Centre, Bull Street - Short Heath) and the pilot scheme was christened "Tracline 65." It rates a mention in this publication because special Autofare 3 rolls (Set A11) were provided.

Fig 4 - Tracline 65 reverse

Tickets were as normal on the front, but on the reverse side carried the inscription "*tracline 65*" in the style of lettering used to promote the service. (Fig 4). "Tracline" tickets were occasionally used (presumably in error) on other routes. Figs 5 and 6 show two Tracline tickets issued on the same bus on the same day, 26th October 1984. The first one is OK, but by 15.53 something had gone wrong. Both the serial number and the machine number had been replaced by hieroglyphics.

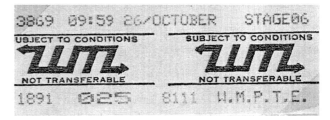

Fig 5

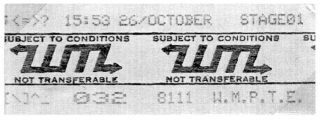

Fig 6

The Guided Busway survived Deregulation, but was abandoned in the Spring of 1987 - a sad end to an interesting (if costly) experiment, and a foretaste of "what might have been."

Collectors will search in vain for Tracline tickets bearing the post-Deregulation West Midlands Travel logo. None were issued.

Return Tickets and Class indications
On 7th January 1985 the PTE launched a new limited stop service 901 between Walsall and Lichfield, using the title "Rapid Rider" - though this name was later discontinued. Off peak Return tickets were available, initially costing £1 (Adult) or 60p (Child). This was interesting because Return fares (which had been available on some of the routes taken over from Midland Red in 1973) were previously abolished in 1974. Buses operating the 901 issued Autofare 3 tickets showing (for the first time) a Class indication, "AR" or "CR."

When the tickets were presented for the return journey, the driver would cancel them with an impressive display of modern fare collection technology. Taking the ticket firmly in both hands, he would smartly tear it in half! A rejoined Return ticket from the 901 is illustrated in Fig 7.

Autofare 1-equipped buses could not, of course, be used on this service. Return tickets were possibly extended to one or two other Limited Stop services, but there was never a general re-introduction of Return fares.

From March 1985, all Autofare 3 tickets showed a Class indication, namely "A" (Adult) or "C" (Child.)

At one stage, WMPTE Autofare 3 tickets were valid on

Fig 7 - Return

Midland Red West buses! Between July and September 1985 the two companies ran a joint service X1 between Brownhills and Bewdley on Sundays and Bank Holiday Monday. Return tickets were available, and the PTE's Autofares tended to show the word "SPECIAL" in place of "W. M. P. T. E." in the bottom right hand corner. (Fig 8). Midland Red West issued their usual Setright tickets, and Returns were available on both operators' buses.

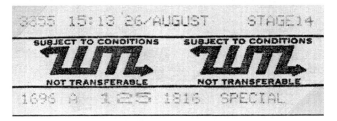

Fig 8 - Joint Service X1 Return

In 1986 the PTE "went it alone" with a service 918 between Stourbridge and Stourport, calling *en route* at the West Midland Safari Park and the Severn Valley Railway Station at Bewdley.

By showing their bus tickets, visitors to the Safari Park could obtain a free admission ticket for a future visit. The 918 ran on Sundays and Bank Holiday Monday / Tuesday from 20th July to 19th October 1986, and Return tickets (standard Autofare 3 issues) were available.

Open Top services

Open top buses are usually associated with breezy seafront services at Rhyl, Bournemouth, Eastbourne, etc., so it is rather surprising that a number of inland operators (including tour operators in London and Stratford upon Avon) have found a use for this kind of bus.

Like most operators of double deckers, WMPTE inevitably suffered the occasional low bridge casualty, and one such victim was ex-Birmingham Daimler Fleetline 3867 (NOV867G), dating from 1968. Having had part of the job done for them (!) they decided to convert it into an open topper for tours and special events. It re-entered service in 1978, after being neatly converted by PTE apprentices. The bus was fitted with a farebox but no ticket machine, and the usual procedure was for passengers to drop the exact fare into the box and travel without a ticket. (In later years, possibly after Deregulation, 3867 received an Autofare 3 machine.)

However, when tours were run in Dudley in 1984, the local garage provided a "real" conductor (last seen in 1980), armed with a "real" ticket machine - namely ex-BMMO Setright

Fig 9 - Dudley Tour

0146, (Fig 9). To transport enthusiasts, this was a welcome touch, and would have been even nicer if special ticket rolls had been used. Instead, they found some Type WM2 rolls. I suspect that a Setright was used by Dudley Garage for tours in 1983 also, but when Walsall Garage used the bus later in 1984, no tickets were issued.

Commencing on 7th April 1985, in connection with Wolverhampton's Millennium celebrations, 3867 was used to run a Sunday afternoon "Civil Wars Heritage Tour" from the local Civic Centre, taking in Boscobel House (where King Charles II hid in the famous oak tree), the nearby Whiteladies Priory, and another royal hiding place, Moseley Old Hall. Special pad tickets were issued - white (Adult) costing £1.80 and yellow (Child / Senior Citizen) 90p. Fares included admission to the houses. The service was run on behalf of Wolverhampton Borough Council, and the tickets were provided by the Council, not WMPTE. No illustration is available, I regret to say.

Another open topper, 4069, later replaced 3867 on this service, which ran until August 1985 and frequently seemed to coincide with wet weather!

Birmingham Ice Rink

In the summer of 1985, visitors to Mecca Leisure's Birmingham Ice Rink could obtain a 50p discount by producing a WMPTE bus or train ticket, Daytripper or Travelcard. Some PTE publicity included a voucher to be presented at the Ice Rink along with the ticket, but the voucher may not have been essential.

Incidentally, Ice Rink admission tickets were large Autofare 3 style issues of the type shown in Fig 10. White with red lines on the front, and the Mecca symbol on the back.

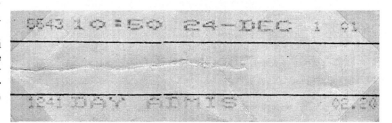

Fig 10 - Birmingham Ice Rink admission

Thrufare

To describe this, I can do no better than to quote from Issue No. 2 of "The WMPTE Traveller," which said, "On July 28th (1985) a new concept in off peak travel was introduced. Known as THRUFARE and costing only 50p, this ticket, which is obtainable from the driver, enables you to take as many off-peak bus rides as you wish in West Midlands County within one hour of purchase. This means that if your last journey starts within one hour of boarding the first bus, you can complete the journey to your destination no matter how far or how long the trip may be."

It was, in a sense, a transfer ticket designed for people who needed to use more than one bus to reach their destination, but could also be used as a Return if time allowed. It was available during the "standard" Off Peak period (9.30 a.m. to 3.30 p.m., 6 p.m. to 11.29 p.m. Mondays to Fridays, and all day until 11.29 p.m. at weekends and Bank Holiday Mondays) and

Fig 11 - Thrufare

was met by issuing a normal Autofare 3 ticket showing "SPECIAL" in the bottom right hand corner. The illustrated specimen (Fig 11) was issued on 1st March 1986, but shows 29th February!

Buses with Autofare 1 sets could not issue Thrufare tickets, and I believe that problems arose when somebody tried to buy one!

Thrufare tickets could not be used on routes 159/900 for journeys crossing Meriden - which claims to be the geographic "centre of England."

A Child Thrufare ticket appears in Fig 12. After Deregulation, West Midlands Travel continued with the scheme.

Fig 12 - Child Thrufare

Shuttlebus
On 14th October 1985 the PTE introduced a minibus service between Pheasey and Old Oscott via Kingstanding, using Ford Transits operating under the title "Shuttlebus." Later, two more services were inaugurated, this time in West Bromwich. Owing to problems with the unions, the services were actually worked by the PTE's coaching subsidiary, Central Coachways of Walsall.

The Old Oscott route had a straightforward flat fare for any distance (initially 20p), whereas the West Bromwich services had a different fare structure, but including a flat fare zone on both routes.

The Shuttlebus venture was interesting to ticket enthusiasts because the 10 minibuses were equipped with Almex machines, understood to be Model P. I believe that the machines were initially rather troublesome, with many tickets appearing in an inky, illegible state. In fact I can reveal that our illustration (Fig 13) had to be slightly doctored to make it more presentable! However, I understand that an Almex technician visited the garage and adjusted the ticket machines, whereupon the problem was solved.

Fig 13 - Almex Model P

Those who have read *Part 1* will know that WMPTE inherited a fairly modest quantity of Almex "A" machines from Birmingham, West Bromwich and Wolverhampton Corporations, but these had all gone by 1976. The 1985 machines were used until Deregulation, and then replaced by Wayfarer IIs.

Perry Barr Open Day
WMPTE garage open days were always enjoyable and well-organised occasions, and the event at their large Perry Barr Garage in Birmingham, on 20th October 1985, was well up to standard.

Not very much in the ticket line on display, though one could buy Walsall "Last Trolleybus" punch tickets (described in *Part 1*) and 1983 Walsall Garage Open Day tickets (see next chapter) from a sales stand run by staff from Walsall District.

However, on another stand, raffle tickets were being sold for charity, and took the form of Autofare 3 tickets on "Tracline" rolls. A machine had been set up to issue them. In the illustrated example (Fig 14) it will be noted that the tickets were programmed to read "PERRY BARR." The bus fleet number shown - 6300 - is fictitious, as the vehicle which bore this number was never fitted with Autofare 3.

Fig 14 - Perry Barr Open Day

Dudley Tourist Bus Service
Between 24th May and 31st August 1986 the PTE operated a tour of the Dudley area at weekends and bank holidays. Not an open top tour this time - there were probably too many low branches *en route*! Perhaps it should be explained that in the present day enthusiasm for promoting tourism in hitherto unlikely places, the Dudley area is regarded as being particularly rich in Black Country "heritage" and industrial archaeology. Somehow, I doubt if they ran tours of the Black Country in the "good old days" of 80 or 100 years ago!

Daytripper and Supertripper tickets were accepted on the 1986 tours, but other passengers had to pay 50p (25p Child) for which they received an Autofare 3 ticket showing "SPECIAL" in place of "W. M. P. T. E." Passengers were given a perforated sheet of 8 vouchers which could be used to obtain discounts at various places *en route*, and they could rejoin the tour on a later bus. For instance, there was 25p off the admission price at the Black Country Museum, a free cup of tea or coffee when visiting a glassworks, or 5p off a pint at the

Fig 15 - Dudley Tourist Bus Service

Park Inn, Woodsetton! The title panel from the voucher sheet is shown in Fig 15. Though obviously not a ticket, this is the kind of small ephemera which collectors may find convenient to keep in their ticket collections.

As far as possible, the Dudley Tourist service was operated by Metrobus 2703 which at that time was painted in an overall "advert" livery to promote the attractions of the area.

West Midlands Travel Autofare 3

On 26th October 1986 WMPTE buses were transferred to a new operator, West Midlands Travel Ltd. The new company's tickets are obviously outside the purview of this publication, but it has to be mentioned that Autofare 3 tickets with the WM Travel logo (blue printing with red shading) made their appearance in some areas a few days before Deregulation. The illustrated example (Fig 16) is dated 23rd October, but I found one dated 19th.

Fig 16 - West Midlands Travel Ltd - Autofare 3

A WMT ticket with "W. M. P. T. E." printed in the bottom right hand corner (as in the illustration) is probably something of a rarity in collections, because after 26th October this was quickly changed to read "WM Travel." The reverse is not the case, because WMPTE Autofare 3s (showing "WM TRAVEL") continued in use for some time after Deregulation.

2   Miscellaneous Tickets

This chapter deals basically with "card or paper" tickets, as opposed to the machine-issued specimens covered in Chapter 1. In addition we have a few "oddities" which do not easily fit in elsewhere. Travelcards need a separate section to themselves, and these appear in Chapter 3.

Tickets which came and went during the 1969-1983 period are dealt with in *Part 2* of this publication, and will not be described again here.

a) Easy Rider

This rather complicated ticket, introduced on 31st August 1980, was fully described in *Part 2*, but basically it was a joint WMPTE / Midland Red (North) ticket valid on the South Staffordshire routes of both operators. It could also be used on certain "corridor" routes from Staffordshire to principal centres in the WM County (Birmingham, Walsall, Dudley and Wolverhampton) but not for journeys wholly within the WM County. Tickets were Adult only, and ran for 4 weeks.

The map (reproduced from a Midland Red North publicity leaflet) shows the area covered by "Easy Rider" (subdivided into Inner and Outer Areas) and also the "corridor" routes.

Fares remained as set out in *Part 2* until 5th November 1983, when the flat fare payable on WMPTE buses was increased from 15p to 16p or from 30p to 32p, as appropriate. This brought them into line with the PTE's normal fare structure and presumably was desirable because the Autofare 3 ticket machines were programmed with these fares.

Midland Red (North) fares were not affected, but the purchase price of an Easy Rider card went up to £7 from the same date.

As shown on the map (overleaf), an extra "zone" was added, whereby passengers travelling to / from the WM County south of Walsall or Aldridge had to pay 45p in the peak period and 32p (30p on Midland Red) at other times.

Issued by the WMPTE and Midland Red (North) Ltd in respect of bus services, subject as may be appropriate to Road Traffic Acts, Public Service Vehicle Regulations and the conditions of the Easy Rider scheme.

Valid only when accompanied by an Easy Rider identity card and may only be used by the person whose portrait appears on the card.

Insofar as this document is an identity card it enables the person to whom it has been issued to travel at a flat fare as set out in publications.

Insofar as this document is a season ticket it enables the person to whom it has been issued to travel without further charge as set out in publications.

Lost tickets not replaced. Not transferable. Easy Rider tickets remain the property of the operators and may be withdrawn if misused. The ticket must be produced to obtain the discount fare or free travel as appropriate. If not so produced, ordinary fares must be paid which are not refundable.

On 25th August 1985, WMPTE Easy Rider fares reverted to 15p and 30p. It seems that they intended to raise the £7 card price at the same time, but the increased price was deleted on the posters which appeared in the buses. However, from 20th April 1986, the price was drastically increased to £8.80.

Following the extension of Travelcard validity to embrace most routes in Staffordshire (see Chapter 3), Easy Rider tickets were abolished by WMPTE on 19th July 1986, but they continued to be sold by Midland Red (North).

If ticket collecting enthusiasts find Easy Rider difficult to understand, what chance was there for the travelling public?!

Three varieties of Easy Rider card are mentioned in *Part 2*. To these must now be added the following:-

iv) price £7.00 Red value figure, as previously.

v) price £7.00 Black value figure, in heavy numerals. (Printed by Booth.)

Presumably there was also an £8.80 version, but I have never seen one, and would welcome confirmation.

And now we can move on to something a little less confusing!

b) Daytripper

These very popular daily "runabout" tickets only just scraped into *Part 2*, as they were introduced on 29th March 1983. No need to describe them in detail again here, but they were "scratch off" tickets (i.e. where the passenger could buy them in advance, and then "scratch off" the date when he used them), valid on all WMPTE buses and on Midland Red buses / BR trains within the WM County.

It is surprising how many people discarded their Daytrippers at railway stations, apparently unaware that they could be used on buses as well.

The original Daytrippers were on stiff card which bent or creased very easily, and I suspect that few collectors have been lucky enough to acquire specimens in perfect condition. Many people folded them in half for easier carrying.

Daytrippers were advertised as being available in three versions:

Family ticket	
(up to 2 adults and 4 children under 16)	Price Code Q
Adult	Price Code QA
Child	Price Code QC

However, collectors will search in vain for a code Q Daytripper on stiff card, because they were never issued. Instead the PTE used up stocks of its predecessor, the Family Day Ticket (also Price Code Q).

In August 1983 they advertised a free ticket offer. "Send 3 used Daytripper tickets of the same value to the address below and we'll send you one similar value ticket absolutely free," said the advert. The offer closed on 5th September.

From 1984, Daytrippers could be purchased at any of the 600 Post Offices in the WM County.

In February 1984 the writer spotted his first Code Q Daytripper, but it was on thin paper rather than stiff card, and was light green with dark green printing. Code QA tickets (light blue with dark blue printing) and QC tickets (pink with red printing) also appeared on thin paper around this time. Depending on the level of stocks held by the various agencies, both "thick" and "thin" Daytrippers could be encountered for a long time afterwards. All tickets showed the same year panels - 1983/4/5, suggesting perhaps that the first tickets may have gone on sale in late 1983 or (more likely) were printed in 1983. By the Spring of 1985, tickets were showing 1984/5/6.

From 14th April until 29th September 1984 (Saturdays

How does Easy Rider Work?

1. Anyone can buy an EasyRider card. You buy it in advance, every four weeks from one of the offices listed in this leaflet (when you buy your first EasyRider, you will need a passport photo and pay a 25p registration fee also).

2. EasyRider costs £7 for four weeks.

3. Once you have your EasyRider card, this entitles you to use red and blue buses at a cheap rate in the area shown opposite.

4. Every time you hop on a bus, show your EasyRider card to the driver and say where you are going. You will then pay NOTHING or A SMALL SUPPLEMENT for your journey, depending upon where you are travelling to and from and the time you make your journey.

5. Look at the map opposite. For a bus journey entirely within the lined Cannock or Lichfield areas (the "inner" areas) you will pay 15 PENCE (WMPTE 16p) on the bus when you use your EasyRider before 9 am and between 3.30 pm and 6 pm on Mondays to Fridays; at all other times*, a bus trip entirely within an "inner" area will cost you NOTHING with EasyRider.

6. For a bus journey within the shaded area (the "outer" area) or crossing to/from an "inner" area you will pay 30 PENCE (WMPTE 32p) on the bus when you use EasyRider before 9 am and between 3.30 pm and 6 pm on Mondays to Fridays; at all other times* your trip will cost you just 15 PENCE (WMPTE 16p) with EasyRider.

7. For journeys from Staffordshire to points in West Midlands County south of Walsall (Bus Station), Aldridge (Elms Hotel) or Little Aston Cross Roads THE SUPPLEMENTARY FARE IS 45 PENCE (up to 9 am and 3.30 pm to 6 pm Mon to Fri), 32 PENCE at other times (30p on Midland Red).

8. If your journey costs money on the bus, the driver will issue you with a ticket to that value — you should keep this to show with your EasyRider Card if an Inspector checks the bus.

9. Remember, with EasyRider your bus journey will cost —

CANNOCK OR LICHFIELD INNER AREAS	up to 9 am and 3.30-6 pm Mon-Fri. — 15 PENCE (WMPTE 16p) all other times* — NOTHING	
STAFFORDSHIRE OUTER AREA & TO WOLVERHAMPTON & WALSALL	up to 9 am and 3.30-6 pm Mon-Fri. — 30 PENCE (WMPTE 32p) all other times* — 15 PENCE (WMPTE 16p).	
STAFFORDSHIRE TO/FROM WEST MIDLANDS SOUTH OF WALSALL, ALDRIDGE, LITTLE ASTON.	Up to 9am and 3.30-6pm Mon to Fri — 45 PENCE all other times — 30 PENCE (WMPTE 32p)	

You can use your EasyRider Card as many times as you wish during its 4-weeks validity*.

*including weekends.

NOV. 1983

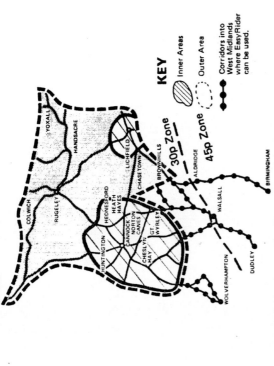

KEY

Inner Areas

Outer Area

Corridors into West Midlands where EasyRider can be used.

the CANNOCK INNER AREA includes Cannock, Hednesford, Heath Hayes, Norton Canes, Great Wyrley, Cheslyn Hay, Bridgtown and Huntington.
the LICHFIELD INNER AREA includes Lichfield City (but is not valid on X12).
the OUTER AREA extends to Stafford, Colwich, Rugeley, Yoxall, Handsacre, Lichfield, Burntwood, Chasetown.
You can also use Easy Rider on buses from Staffordshire to Wolverhampton, Walsall, Dudley and Birmingham (but not X30/1 motorway service south of the M6 junction at Laney Green or X12) — precise points of availability and services are available from offices and agents.
EASYRIDERS are NOT valid for journeys wholly in West Midlands County.

Where to Buy Easy Rider

Initial ticket purchases and renewals—
CANNOCK—Midland Red Travel Centre, Delta Way, Bridgtown.
STAFFORD—Midland Red Garage, Pilgrim Place, off Newport Road.
LICHFIELD—Midland Red Office, Bus Station.
WOLVERHAMPTON—WMPTE Office, Cleveland Road.
WALSALL—WMPTE Office, St. Paul's Street.

Renewals (only)—
HEDNESFORD—Likeman, 101A Market Street.
RUGELEY—The Post Office, 55 Horsefair.
LICHFIELD—Pathfinder Travel, Bore Street.
CANNOCK—Simmons, Newsagents, 30 Stafford Road and Bus Station Kiosk.
CHASETOWN—Hardwick, Post Office, 13 High Street.
BURNTWOOD—Jones "The Toy Shop", 22 Cannock Road.
HEATH HAYES—Post Office or Heath Hayes Travel.
PYE GREEN—Sunbeam Stores, 81 Broadhurst Green.

West Midlands PTE / Midland Red (North) - Easy Rider

Daytripper - Family

Daytripper - Child

Daytripper - Adult

only, plus Wednesdays in school holidays) Reading Transport operated a Route X3 (Reading - Stratford upon Avon - Birmingham) and they reached agreement with WMPTE for Daytrippers to be sold at a discount price at their Mill Lane office, to passengers booking seats on the X3. They were not, of course, valid on the X3 itself, but could be used by passengers when they reached Birmingham.

From May 1985 the PTE were able to extend the rail validity of Daytrippers to certain stations outside the WM County i.e. to Lichfield, Leamington Spa, Stratford and intermediate stations on the lines from Birmingham. Initially, publicity leaflets also showed the mainly single track Coventry - Leamington line (reopened to passenger trains in 1976) but BR quickly made it clear that Daytrippers were not valid on this line. Rail validity outside the WM County was, however, withdrawn in May 1986 when the Supertripper (q.v.) was introduced.

A photographic competition was announced in May 1985, the idea being that Daytripper-users could enter photos taken on their travels. All entries had to be accompanied by a Daytripper or Southern Rider (q.v.), and a Family Daytripper entitled people to two entries. Various attractive photographic prizes were offered, and finalists were to be judged by the well known photographer Patrick Lichfield. Associated with this, but not restricted to competition entrants, was a film processing offer, whereby one could receive a discount on processing by sending a used Daytripper or Southern Rider with the film. Send 3 tickets and your film was processed free.

After Deregulation in 1986, Daytrippers were perpetuated by the new company, West Midlands Travel, but were no longer valid on other companies' buses.

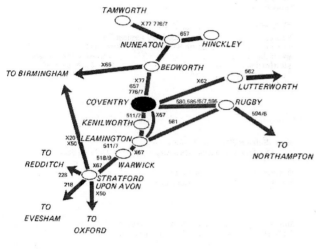

GET OUT AND ABOUT WITH A

COVENTRY & WARWICKSHIRE
DAY OUT TICKET

GIVING UNLIMITED TRAVEL FOR A DAY ON WEST MIDLAND PTE (COVENTRY) AND MIDLAND RED SOUTH SERVICES.

NOW AVAILABLE THROUGHOUT THE YEAR.

BUY ONE TICKET AND CATCH AS MANY BUSES AS YOU LIKE

LOOK AT THE PLACES YOU CAN VISIT:—

Fig 17 - Coventry and Warwickshire Day Out

The Coventry and Warwickshire Day Out Area

c) Coventry & Warwickshire Day Out

Now we move on to a completely new range of "scratch off" card tickets, introduced in July 1983. Initially they were only available until September, but were continued indefinitely. Rather similar to Daytrippers in general layout (see Fig 17), they were a joint promotion by WMPTE East Division (i.e. Coventry) and Midland Red (South) Ltd. Tickets could be used on all PTE services in Coventry (except those to Birmingham and Solihull) and on all but a handful of MR(S) services (X67/8, 640, 658). Timing restrictions were identical to Daytrippers.

"Where can I purchase my Day Out ticket?" asks the publicity leaflet, and then answers its own question by saying, *"Buy it in advance from the West Midlands or Midland Red South Travel Centres in Coventry, Pool Meadow Bus Station ..."* Three versions were available:

Family ticket	Price Code QW	brown
Adult ticket	Price Code QX	pink
Child ticket	Price Code QY	gold

Year panels showed 1983/4/5. Prices of these and other tickets in this chapter are set out in Appendix A. These tickets were superseded by Southern Rider tickets which were introduced on 25th May 1985.

d) Walsall Garage Open Day ticket

A very "rare" ticket - but only rare in the sense that (unlike most) they were issued free of charge! The tickets themselves are easy enough to obtain.

On 24th July 1983, WMPTE held an Open Day at their garage and works in Walsall, and the public turned up in droves. Many people arrived on the free "park and ride" service operated between the town centre and the garage, using numerous "advert buses" borrowed from different garages in the North and South divisions.

It was on these buses that these rather neat light blue tickets (Fig 18) were handed out to passengers. The smiling cartoon character is, of course, the PTE's jovial mascot 'Wumpty' who appeared in many publicity leaflets, sometimes exchanging his driver's cap for different headgear to suit the occasion. The back of the ticket is blank.

Fig 18 - Walsall Garage Open Day - Souvenir Ticket

11

A "programmed" Autofare 3 machine and a Farespeed were being demonstrated to visitors in the former trolleybus depot. Examples of the tickets issued are shown in Figs 19 and 20 respectively. Farespeed was never used by WMPTE in public service.

Fig 19 - Walsall Garage Open Day - Autofare 3

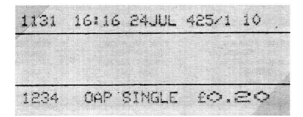

Fig 20- Walsall Garage Open Day - Farespeed

e) Airlink

Old pieces of furniture sometimes have secret drawers; old houses may have secret passages. The old PTE had what was almost a "secret" ticket - and this is it!

Airlink was similar in general terms to a Daytripper, but could only be purchased at Birmingham Airport and was intended for use by people arriving in the West Midlands by air. In contrast to Daytrippers, which have been plugged almost to saturation point, Airlink tickets

were rarely mentioned in print, no information leaflet seemed to be available, and few members of staff seemed to know anything at all about them!

As the illustration (Fig 21) shows, they were "scratch off" tickets, and were available for travel on all WMPTE buses without exception, plus Midland Red buses / BR trains in the WM County.

Validity differed from Daytrippers in two noteworthy ways:

1) There were no timing restrictions whatsoever.
2) They could be used on the Birmingham Night Services.

Purchasers received a sealed package containing a WMPTE route map, various timetable leaflets and an introductory leaflet in 3 languages. These information packs were not, it seems, updated.

Airlink tickets appear to have been introduced in the Autumn of 1983 (even the date is secret!) and were withdrawn at the end of 1985 when their year panels (1983/4/5) expired. Was I the last person to use one, in December 1985, I wonder?

My ticket was actually purchased in May 1985, and its low serial number (000033) suggested that very few had been sold during the previous 18 months or so. All the literature in the pack was of 1983 vintage. As far as I know, there was no Child version of Airlink.

f) Rotary Travelcard.

Despite its name, the Rotary Travelcard was not a member of the well known family of WMPTE Travelcard season tickets. It was very much a "one off," valid for just one week, 1st - 7th June 1984.

During the above week, the Rotary Organisation held their International Convention at the National Exhibition Centre near Birmingham, and this special ticket was provided by WMPTE for the use of delegates. It was sent to them in advance of their arrival, accompanied by a folded leaflet showing suggested places for visiting. Tickets were valid as shown in the illustrations (Fig 22 and 23), and it is interesting to note that Rotary Travelcards could be used on Midland Red (South) buses between Coventry, Warwick and Leamington Spa. This was the second WMPTE ticket which was usable on MR(S) buses outside the WM County, and we shall meet another one later.

Fig 21 - Airlink

Fig 22 - Rotary Travelcard

CONDITIONS OF ISSUE

1. Valid for travel on all W.M.P.T.E. and Midland Red service buses and trains within the West Midlands County as set out in W.M.P.T.E. and B.R. publications and Midland Red South Services between Coventry, Warwick and Leamington.
2. Does not give priority over other passengers.
3. Refunds not made.
4. Lost tickets not replaced.
5. Not transferable.

This ticket may be retained as a souvenir

Issued subject to British Rail Bye Laws, Publications and Notices and to the published terms and conditions relating to the Executives services and facilities which are available for inspection at Divisional Offices at 16 Summer Lane, Birmingham, St Pauls Street, Walsall and Harnall Lane East, Coventry and subject to the conditions of carriage and passenger regulations of Midland Red South details of which are available from Head Office, Railway Terrace, Rugby.

Fig 23 - Rotary Travelcard - reverse

Rotary Travelcards were not, of course, free! They were sold by WMPTE as part of a transport "package" which included ferrying a very large number of Rotarians between their hotels (in such far apart places as Shrewsbury, Cheltenham and Derby) and the NEC.

Although not mentioned on the tickets themselves, the brochure seemed to indicate validity on certain Midland Red (North) routes outside the WM County, serving such places as Cannock Chase and Lichfield.

g) Leisure Rider

"Under sixteen and living in Wolverhampton?" said the advertisement in the "Express & Star" newspaper on 16th July 1984. "From 1st - 25th August, a Leisure Rider card allows you free use of many of Wolverhampton's modern sport and leisure facilities and free WMPTE off-peak travel within the Borough, Monday to Saturday for just £2" (per week.)

The ticket was a joint promotion by the Borough Council and WMPTE, and was an attempt to reduce boredom (and the problems caused by it) during the long summer holidays.

In practice, tickets were available from Monday 30th July, and were obtainable on Fridays or Saturdays from Bilston Leisure Centre, Wednesfield Library and Penn Library, or (on Fridays only) from the Town Clerk's Dept at Wolverhampton Civic Centre. They were not obtainable from WMPTE offices or agents.

I was unable to acquire one of these tickets, but I understand that they were simply WMPTE Child Off-Peak Travelcards (Price Code OB) with a Council stamp or sticker applied to them.

Applicants were required to take along a colour passport size photograph or (if they had one) a WMPTE bus pass identity card of the type used with Scholars Tickets and Travelcards. Leisure Cards could be used during the "standard" off-peak period (Monday to Saturdays) but were not usable on Sundays.

h) Staffordshire Police Activity & Community Enterprise (SPACE)

This ticket was very similar in purpose to the previous one. It was not issued by WMPTE but was valid on their buses, in Staffordshire only. During the school summer holidays

in 1984, Staffordshire Police ran a community scheme for children, and one of these pale green tickets was issued to each child taking part. They entitled the participants to travel on bus services within the county at a maximum fare of 20p. A photograph of the holder had to be affixed.

No fewer than 15 very assorted operators agreed to accept these tickets on their buses - 5 NBC companies, 9 independents and WMPTE. The printers seem to have gone through a "bad spell". The name of the latter operator is rendered as WEST MIALDANDS TRANSPORT! "Midland Red Fox" also looks very dubious (perhaps they were getting mixed up with the "quick brown fox" who jumped over the lazy dog), whilst "Proctors" should be "Procters"!

These illustrations (Figs 24 and 25) are reduced in size, and taken from the TTS *Journal* for October 1984. Full size was 15cm x 10.3cm. No details are known, but similar tickets may have been issued in subsequent years.

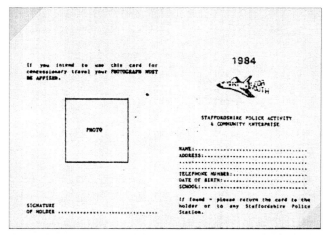

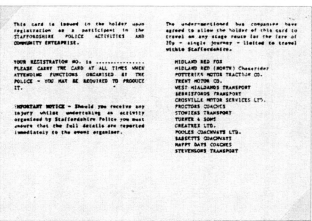

Fig 24 and 25 - Staffordshire Police Activity & Community Enterprise

j) Motor Show, 1984

For the fourth time in succession, the biennial Motor Show was held at the N. E. C. in October 1984 (from 20th - 28th). "Standard" travel / admission tickets (Fig 26) were on sale, giving return bus / train travel to the NEC from any point in the WM County, plus admission to the Show. Details were as follows:

	Adult	Child
Monday - Friday	£3.25 red	£2.90 green
Sat / Sun	£2.75 buff	£2.40 blue

For Travelcard holders, and those with Pensioners passes, admission prices were £2.50 (Mon - Fri) and £2 (Sat / Sun), with no reduction for Child Travelcards.

To add a bit of interest to the proceedings, WMPTE were running a competition whereby visitors could take a

Fig 26 - Motor Show 1984

Fig 27 - Motor Show 1984 - Magic Card

"Magic Card" (Fig 27), obtainable from PTE and BR enquiry offices, along to a stand on the concourse at Birmingham International Station (adjoining the NEC), where a "magic pen" would be run over it to reveal what they had won! First prize was a holiday in France, but every entrant was guaranteed to "win" a Cadbury's "Double Decker" chocolate bar worth 16p in the shops!

Nothing to do with tickets (nor even with WMPTE) but during 1984 a Maglev transport system was opened between International Station and the nearby Birmingham Airport. This consisted of 2 elevated tracks on which passenger cars "ran" by magnetic levitation. The car was lifted by electro magnets and then moved along by a linear motor. Quite a good speed was achieved, but the opening of the line (timed for April 1984) was delayed by technical problems. The Maglev ran fitfully from about July 1984 onwards, and was brought into full time service from the Motor Show period. Three cars were available, but normally only two (and sometimes only one) were operated. Occasionally, two cars ran in tandem. Travelling was free, with no tickets being issued. Sadly, the Maglev was closed down some years ago.

For other public exhibitions at the NEC, WMPTE continued to sell combined travel / admission tickets which were advertised in the press and on the buses. As far as I know, these always took the form of "standard" tickets. No special designs are known during the 1983-6 period.

k) Southern Rider
Another very interesting ticket, introduced on 25th May 1985. Similar to Daytrippers in many ways, Southern Riders were usable on all WMPTE bus services, plus

Midland Red buses and BR second class trains within the WM County, and also on most Midland Red (South) bus services outside the County. Thus it was possible to use a WMPTE ticket many miles outside the range of WMPTE buses. A small number of MR(S) services were excluded, mainly those serving the Leicester area. Southern Riders were not valid on rail services outside the WM County. Timing restrictions were the same as Daytrippers, except that tickets were usable on MR(S) buses from 9.00 a.m. instead of 9.30. Three versions were available:

Family ticket	Price Code QF(?)	Brown
Adult ticket	Price Code QD	Orange. (Fig 28.)
Junior ticket	Price Code QE(?)	Purple

Tickets could be purchased from WMPTE Travel Centres, and from MR(S) Travel Shops in Coventry, Stratford, Leamington, Banbury, Nuneaton and Rugby. An attractive publicity leaflet was produced, showing an artist's drawing of a WMPTE Metrobus, MR(S) Olympian coach and a BR DMU on the front, with photographs inside of places to visit.

As with Daytrippers, some places offered a discount on admission charges. These included Birmingham Railway Museum, The Black Country Museum and the National Motorcycle Museum near the NEC.

Southern Rider tickets were withdrawn from sale in 1986, and the writer may have been one of the last people to use one.

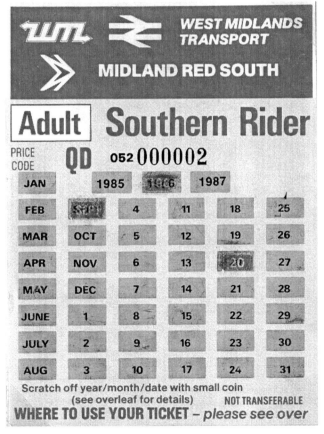

Fig 28- Southern Rider

l) London Liner
This was the name given to an express coach service between Birmingham (Colmore Row) and London (Wilton Road, Victoria) introduced on 17th March 1986 and jointly operated by WMPTE's coaching subsidiary Central Coachways and London Buses Ltd. Initially there were 8 journeys per day each way at 2-hourly intervals.

Tickets were "large paper" specimens (Fig 29), bookable in advance, and with details hand written. On

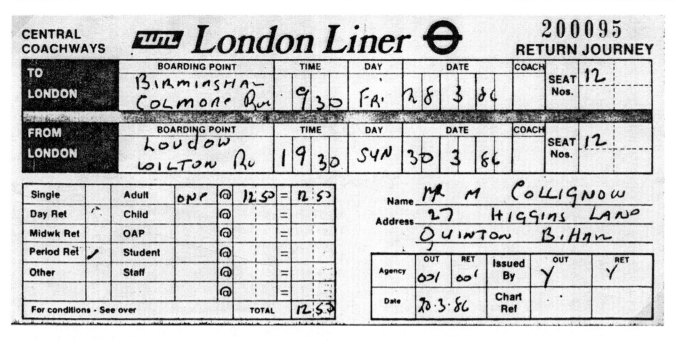

Fig 29 - London Liner - Central Coachways issue

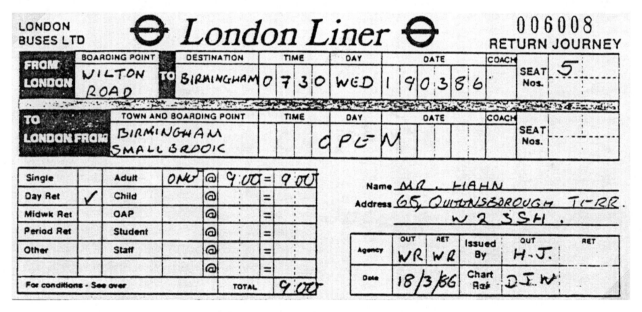

Fig 30 - London Liner - London Buses issue

PTE-issued tickets the Outward portion was blue and the Return red. Designers were RTA Advertising of Acocks Green, Birmingham.

Although very similar, the LBL-issued tickets were slightly different (Fig 30) and made no mention of WMPTE in their title. In this case the Outward portion was red, and the Return was blue.

When the service commenced, Central Coachways ran a brace of bulbous fronted Bovas, whilst LBL used a duo of Duple bodied DAFs, but by June 1986 both operators were using massive MCW Metroliner 3-axle double deckers.

The London Liner service was continued by West Midlands Travel after Deregulation, but London Buses later dropped out, leaving WMT to go it alone.

m) Supertripper

In mid-May 1986, a brand new "scratch off" ticket unexpectedly appeared. This was the Supertripper, which was really an extended version of the Daytripper.

Supertripper embraced all the validity and conditions of the Daytripper, but was additionally valid on several sections of railway outside the WM County, namely to or from Cosford, Penkridge, Lichfield, Water Orton, Leamington (Birmingham line), Stratford, Redditch and Kidderminster. Tickets could also be used on the Coventry - Leamington line, but not on Saturdays between 24th May and 30th August 1986 inclusive.

Four versions were available, including (for the first time) a Senior Citizen issue, which could only be used in conjunction with a WMPTE Pensioners Pass or BR Senior Citizens Railcard. Tickets were as follows: (Figs 31-33)

Family	£4.50	Price Code QG	Mauve
Adult	£2.25	Price Code QH	Light brown / cream
Junior	£1.25	Price Code QJ	Pink
Senior Citizen	£1.25	Price Code QK	Dark Green

Supertrippers could be purchased at all WMPTE travel centres, agencies and BR stations in the WM County, plus

Fig 31 - Supertripper - Adult

Fig 33 - Supertripper - reverse

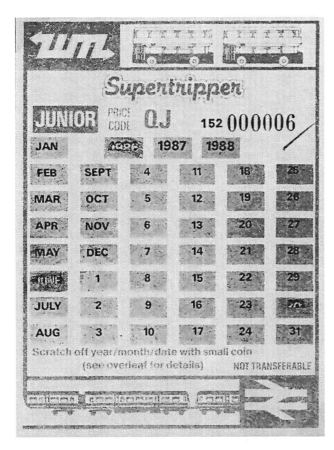

Fig 32 - Supertripper - Junior

16 railway stations outside the County, on the appropriate sections of line. The introduction of Supertrippers meant that Daytrippers could no longer be used on trains outside the WM County.

A colourful brochure, covering both types of ticket, was published in May 1986.

n) Blind or Disabled Persons Free Travel Pass
These passes were valid on all bus services within the WM County and on certain specified sections of route outside the County. No time limits were stipulated.

Full details are not available, but it is clear that the format of these passes changed over the years. Fig 34 shows a 1974 pass, which was yellow with a red diagonal stripe.

Fig 34 - Free Travel Pass

Fig 35 - Blind/Disabled Person Free Travel Pass

Fig 37 - Representatives Pass

The 1977 version measured 3½" x 2½" and was on stiff yellow card with black text printed across the longer dimension, i.e. horizontal format. There was a red band overprint.

The 1978 version was in vertical format, with the red band omitted.

Our second illustration, Fig 35 is taken from a WMPTE staff leaflet dated December 1984. Colour was yellow with a red top.

The final type prior to Deregulation (and still issued afterwards) is the identity card shown in Fig 36. This was used in conjunction with an Annual Travelcard, and mentions validity on trains, which some earlier examples did not. I am grateful to Brian Baker for kindly providing this illustration.

Fig 36 - Disabled Person Identity Card

o) Representatives Pass

This type of pass was issued to people undertaking temporary work on the PTE's behalf (e.g. survey work) but who did not qualify for staff free travel. The illustrated specimen (Fig 37) was on orange card with crimson text.

Next we feature two British Rail tickets which qualify for a mention here because of their obvious WMPTE connotations.

p) Bus Transfer Supplementary Ticket

This blue Edmondson type railway ticket (Fig 38) was issued to visiting Tottenham Hotspur supporters on 24th March 1984 for use on a connecting bus between Coventry Station and Highfield Road football ground. The illustration is taken from the July 1985 TTS *Journal*.

Holders of these tickets were already in possession of a BR Charter Control ticket valid for rail travel to and from Coventry.

Fig 38 - Bus Transfer Supplementary Ticket

q) Marston Green Almex

This ticket rates a mention because of its dual BR / WMPTE title. Issue No. 2 of the "WMPTE Traveller" publicity newspaper included a photograph of a self service Almex Ticfak 4000-8 ticket machine (on loan from the manufacturers) which had been experimentally installed at Marston Green station in the south eastern suburbs of Birmingham. The machine was programmed to issue tickets to New Street only, in 3 varieties: Single, Return or Off Peak Return, both Adult and Child.

It will be seen from Fig 39 that the words "MARSTON GREEN TO BIRMINGHAM NEW STREET" were preprinted on the tickets. Lettering was green, with machine printed data in violet ink, and the serial number

*Fig 39 - Marston Green Station
- Almex Ticfak*

in red. The following "Ticket Type" codes were used:

	Adult	Child
Single	A1	C1
Return	A2	C2
Off Peak Return	A3	C3

r) City Sightseeing Tour

On Wednesdays and Sundays from 1st October until 16th November 1986, a guided tour of Birmingham city centre was operated, using one of the new Metrobus dual purpose double deckers. (Not a Metroliner, as stated in the publicity leaflet.)

With Deregulation taking place on 26th October, the tours began under WMPTE auspices, and ended under the new West Midlands Travel. In fact the publicity leaflet (although issued well before Deregulation) showed the new WMT title and logo, and was one of the first to do so.

The venture was jointly sponsored with the Birmingham Convention and Visitors Bureau, and it appears that the latter people organised the tickets, which were on thin card, and did not carry the WMPTE or WMT title.

The inscription at the top of the tickets is very small, but reads "BIRMINGHAM / The big heart of England." (see figs 40 and 41) Three types of ticket were produced:

Adult	£2.00 yellow
Child, Student, Senior Citizen, Adult with Daytripper/Supertripper	£1.50 blue
Child or Senior Citizen with Daytripper/Supertripper	£1.00 orange

The blue ticket must have broken records for the number of different classes that it covered!

Tours started by the Rotunda office block overlooking St. Martins Circus (the tall cylindrical building depicted on the short-lived Short Distance Travelcards of 1980/1) and took about 1½ hours to show passengers the city's industrial, religious, architectural and social "heritage" etc.

These were by no means the first tours of Birmingham. The City Transport Dept ran tours as long ago as 1966, using new Daimler Fleetlines. They found that Brummies outnumbered visitors on the tours, and I suspect that the same was probably true in 1986!

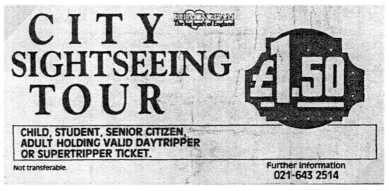

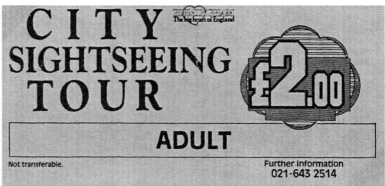

*Figs 40 and 41 -
City Sightseeing Tour*

s) Motor Show 1986

Ending on Deregulation day itself, the 1986 Motor Show was held at the NEC and was open to the public from 18th - 26th October. WMPTE advertised "Free wheeler" tickets covering bus / train travel plus admission - but these turned out to be nothing more exciting than the "standard" tickets which had remained unchanged in design since 1977 at least!

Details were as follows:

Adult	£3.70	red
Child	£3.00	green

Evidence suggests that the "standard" tickets were produced by two different printers.

Summary.

To the transport enthusiast who collects tickets, one of the problems with WMPTE tickets is understanding the different permutations of validity and restrictions. Some were valid on all PTE routes, some only within the WM County, some on trains and some on buses only, some in specified areas or at specified times, etc, etc. If the ticket collector gets confused, it's hardly surprising that the passenger does too!

The following table tries to set out (in simplified form) the differing validity of the main types of "miscellaneous tickets" used between 1969 and 1986. Bearing in mind that some of them changed their validity over the years, the table shows the situation at 25th Oct 1986 or (where applicable) when the ticket was withdrawn from sale.

Columns are numbered 1-14, as follows:

1   Duration of ticket.
2   "Scratch-off" ticket?
3   Holders photo required?

Valid on:

4   All WMPTE routes (except Birmingham Night Services.)
5   All WMPTE routes (except Birmingham Night Services) in WM County.
6   Specified WMPTE routes outside WM County.
7   WMPTE routes within WM County, subject to geographical restrictions.

8   Birmingham Night Services. (Travelcard holders paid half-fare.)
9   Midland Red routes within WM County.
10   Specified Midland Red routes outside WM County.
11   All or specified BR services within WM County.
12   Specified BR routes outside WM County.
13   Subject to timing restrictions?
14   Still available up to 25 Oct 1986, and continued by West Midlands Travel Ltd. after deregulation. (N.B. In most cases, validity was modified under WMT.)

	1	2	3	4	5	6	7	8	9	10	11	12	13	14
Family Ticket (1970) *	1 day			✓										
Easy Rider	4 weeks		✓	✓		✓	✓		✓	✓			✓	
Family Day Ticket *	1 day	✓		✓					✓	✓	✓		✓	
Daytripper	1 day	✓		✓					✓		✓		✓	✓
Coventry & Warwicks Day Out	1 day	✓				✓	✓		✓	✓			✓	
Airlink	1 day	✓		✓				✓	✓		✓			
Southern Rider	1 day	✓		✓					✓	✓	✓		✓	
Supertripper	1 day	✓		✓					✓		✓	✓	✓	✓
Countywide Travelcard	Various		✓	✓				✓	✓		✓			✓
Area Travelcard	1 or 4 wks	✓				✓	✓		✓		✓			✓
Off Peak Travelcard	2 weeks	✓	✓						✓		✓		✓	✓
Off Peak Area TravelCard	2 weeks	✓				✓	✓		✓		✓		✓	✓
Pensioners Pass	Unlimited	✓			✓				✓		✓		✓	✓

* Described in *Tickets of the West Midlands PTE, 1969-1983, Part 2.*

3   Travelcards

Everyone in the West Midlands knows what Travelcards are - or they should do, after the extensive publicity given to this range of season tickets!

The long and very complicated story of Travelcards, from their inception in 1972 up to March 1983 is told in *Part 3* of *"Tickets of the West Midlands PTE,"* but it might be a good idea to include a brief resumé here. Nearly every year since 1972 has seen at least one important development, with plenty of minor ones in between.

The first Travelcards were in a "horizontal format," and went on sale in October 1972. They were 4-weekly tickets valid only on WMPTE buses and available for Adults or Children. Weekly tickets came out in September 1973, with 13-weekly and 10-weekly ones added in later years. 1975 was a "big year," with validity extended first to Midland Red buses and later to BR train services (in both cases restricted to within the WM County). However the same year also saw the withdrawal of Travelcard validity from PTE routes in Staffordshire, followed by the County of Hereford and Worcester in 1976.

From 1st April 1979 the shape of Travelcards changed to the "vertical format" style which remained in use until Deregulation. Price Codes first appeared in August of that year. 1980 saw the introduction of "Area Travelcards" in Wolverhampton and Coventry (plus Walsall in 1981) but the main development of 1980 was the "rationalisation" which simplified the range of Travelcards on sale, and did away with separate tickets for "Bus Only," "Bus plus One Rail Line" etc. Henceforth, all Travelcards (subject to the geographical restrictions of the Area cards) were valid on all bus and rail services within the County, plus the very small mileage outside the County in the Frankley area (south west of Birmingham.)

Countywide "Off Peak" Travelcards were added to the range in 1982. These were valid outside peak travelling periods, and gave a considerable saving in cost.

It is not possible to give a definitive list of Travelcard varieties actually on sale on 1st April 1983 - the date on which this volume commences - because some Agencies may still have been selling obsolete varieties until stocks were used up. However, the *basic* range was as follows:

Price Code	Type	Design Reference Number (See Part 3)
F	Child, 4 weeks	Tc295
G	Adult, 4 weeks	Tc260, 260A, 262*
L	Adult, 1 week	Tc267, 267A
M	Child, 1 week	Tc269, 270, 270A
U	Student, 10 weeks	Tc280, 281*
W	Adult, 13 weeks	Tc292, 292A*
BE	Coventry, Adult, 4 weeks	Tc322
BK	Coventry, Adult, 1 week	Tc325, 326, 326A
CE	Wolverhampton, Adult, 4 weeks	Tc341A, 342
CK	Wolverhampton, Adult, 1 week	Tc345A, 346
DE	Walsall, Adult, 4 weeks	Tc361
DK	Walsall, Adult, 1 week	Tc365
OA	Off Peak, Adult, 2 weeks	Tc403
OB	Off Peak, Child, 2 weeks	Tc402, 404(?)

* First listed in this Publication.

New varieties introduced after 1st April 1983 (and earlier varieties "discovered" after this date) are listed in a table at the end of this chapter. A composite list of prices appears in Appendix A.

On 8th August 1983 a new style of identity card, known as a "Photocard" was introduced. This incorporated a colour photo of the holder, and more details are given in Chapter 5.

People with the 1980-style Data Cards (with black and white photographs) were not required to change them,

however. Photocards were now issued to all *new* Travelcard holders and (from the Autumn Term of 1983) were also required to be used with Scholars Tickets.

An "off peak fare" system was introduced on 2nd October 1983 (see Chapter 1 for more details) and the price of Off Peak Travelcards was reduced from this date. Other Travelcard prices were not affected.

After 4 February 1984, the original 1972-style of Travelcard identity card was no longer accepted for renewals. These should have been replaced in 1980 by Data Cards, but many people did not bother to have them changed, and renewal offices continued to accept the old type.

An interesting venture during July and August 1984 was the "Costclipper" discount scheme, whereby Travelcard holders could obtain a variety of discounts on purchases made at certain shops in Wolverhampton.

"To obtain your 'COSTCLIPPER' bargains, just present your valid current Travelcard, area Travelcard or off peak Travelcard at the shop ..." said the publicity brochure. *"Watch for the Costclipper posters identifying participating shops and SAVE EVEN MORE WHEN YOU BUY TRAVELCARD."*

About 70 shops or other business premises were listed in the brochure, ranging from chain stores like Boot's and Woolworths down to suburban grocers, fish shops etc. Some shops offered a certain percentage off all purchases, but others stipulated particular products or ranges. British Rail were offering reductions on Midland Railtourer tickets, but these had to be purchased from WMPTE's Cleveland Road office. Do these count (albeit very loosely!) as WMPTE tickets? They carried the PTE's name and address as the place of issue. See Fig 42.

The PTE themselves were offering free photocards (value 35p) to all new Travelcard applicants.

Commencing on 5th November 1984, WMPTE "launched" (to use the word currently in vogue) a major advertising campaign to promote the sale of Travelcards, reputedly costing £120,000, and using the slogan "Do the hop." Publicity leaflets were delivered to 937,000 households in the WM County during the two weeks commencing 12th November. A total of 15 peak and 20 off peak 30 second "spots" on Central TV and 30 "spots" on Channel 4 were booked for the weeks commencing 5th November to 3rd December, and 105 x 30 second adverts were broadcast on each of BRMB, Beacon and Mercia Sound radio stations during the weeks commencing 12th, 19th and 26th November. Added to this was a large range of advertisements in 6 local newspapers plus 50 T-shape bus side adverts, 50 upper rear space bus adverts and 5,000 A4-size window bills. Finally, there were 300 posters and 400 vinyl stickers for display by agents and railway stations etc. The campaign was timed to finish on 3rd December, but some of the bus adverts could still be seen long after this date, and the "Do the hop" slogan was re-used on later Travelcard publicity.

The advertising firm who handled the campaign on behalf of the PTE was Charles Barker, Black and Gross of Birmingham.

It was possible for rail travellers to buy "Add On" Travelcards, which consisted of a normal Travelcard for use inside the WM County, plus a BR season ticket for through travel on lines which crossed the County boundary. The latter would be valid for the same duration as the Travelcard - 1, 4 or 13 weeks, and was really intended for people who lived in Staffordshire, Shropshire or Warwickshire and who travelled regularly into the WM County (or vice versa.) An example issued for use on the Birmingham - Lichfield line was illustrated in *Part 3* of *"Tickets of the West Midlands PTE."*

An Annual Travelcard was introduced on 2nd January 1985, and the first 3,000 applicants, including this writer received a free bound "A-Z" for the West Midlands area.

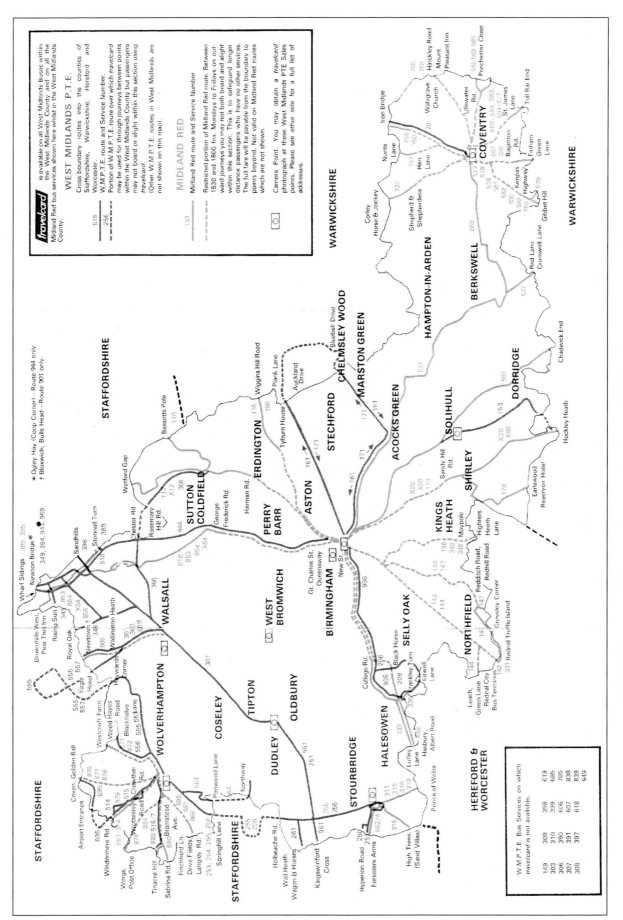

WMPTE Map showing limits of Travelcard validity and other conditions - August 1977

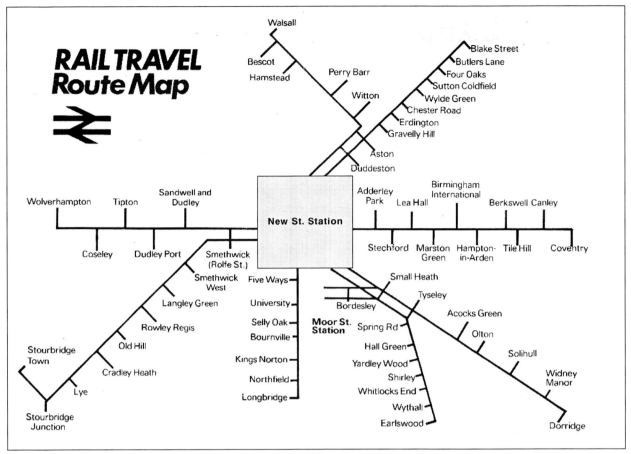

British Rail lines and stations within the WMPTE Travelcard area

From April 1985, holders of Bus / Rail Annual Travelcards were able to purchase an Annual Season Ticket Holders Railcard from BR, entitling them to reductions on Cheap Day Returns and Savers.

On 27th October 1985 WMPTE issued a new Off Peak Travelcard for use in Coventry only, i.e. an Off Peak version of the Coventry Travelcard introduced in 1980. From the same date, the price of the latter tickets was slightly increased making them more expensive than the Wolverhampton and Walsall Travelcards. Hitherto, the prices in all three areas had been the same. However, when fares were increased on 6th April 1986, prices were once again standardised.

Momentous changes took place in November 1985, when Travelcard validity was reinstated on most (if not all) of the Staffordshire sections of route radiating from Wolverhampton. Perhaps it was intended as a "sweetener" to atone for the fact that (from 24 November 1985) some of those areas suffered reductions in service! As mentioned elsewhere, Travelcards had been previously withdrawn from Staffordshire routes with effect from 11th May 1975 and from routes in the County of Hereford and Worcester from 3rd October 1976. Validity was fully restored to the latter region in November 1985. The exact date of restoration was not apparently publicised, but seems to have been 24th November in all cases.

In April 1986 (again, the precise date seems uncertain but was probably 6th) Off Peak Area Travelcards were introduced in Wolverhampton and Walsall. On the publicity leaflet, a rosy cheeked Town Crier announced "Great news for all ye citizens of the above towns." As with the earlier Coventry Off Peak Travelcard, prices were £2.60 for 2 weeks, and timing restrictions were in line with the Countywide Off Peak cards.

Another momentous day was Sunday 29th June 1986, when Travelcard validity was reinstated on Staffordshire routes running from Walsall, and also on the Kinver service (on the Stourbridge flank of the WM County.) Following the events of November '85, this meant that Travelcards were once again valid on all (or virtually all) sections of route outside the WM County.

On the same date the Walsall Area and Walsall Off Peak Travelcards were extended to include Cannock.

These developments will be regarded as WMPTE's "response" to Midland Red (North), who introduced a network of Chaserider minibuses in the Cannock area the same weekend. In the run-up to Deregulation, MR(N) was seen as a strong competitor on the South Staffordshire "front," although in the event things did not work out that way.

"What's Happening to Travelcards?" was the heading of a WMPTE press advertisement in September 1986 - using, incidentally, the new West Midlands Travel logo.

"You can still buy the existing 1 week, 4 week, 10 week and Off peak Travelcards up to 21 October," said the advert.

"Existing holders of Annual Travelcards can renew them but they will not be available for first-time purchasers from 24 September to 22 October. Adult 13 week tickets will be withdrawn from sale after 23 September.

After 22 October you can buy the new West Midlands Travel Travelcards for 1 week, 4 weeks, 10 weeks, or a year. Also Off Peak Travelcards and Young Persons Travelcards. Travelcards for use on WM Travel buses only will cost the same as existing Travelcards - Bus / Rail Travelcards will be at a higher price.

All existing Travelcards of WMPTE and new Travelcards of WM Travel will be accepted on WM Travel buses and, where relevant, on local trains as long as they are valid."

This seems to sum up, quite adequately, the Travelcard situation during the last few weeks before Deregulation (or Derelegation, as one bus driver called it, when talking to the writer!)

Travelcard Issues April 1983 - October 1986

(Including some slightly earlier issues not shown in *Part 3*).

Design	Price code	Weeks	Adult Child or Student	Approximate date of first issue	SA	SB	Back block	See note	
Tc262	G	4	A			✓	O.P.	2	
Tc281	U	10	S		✓	✓	Q	3	
Tc292	W	13	A			✓	U		
Tc292A	W	13	A	c Sep 83		✓	R	1	
Tc293	W	13	A	83		✓	Q	10	
Tc296	F	4	C	c Oct 83	✓	✓	Q	4	
Tc322A	BE	4	A				C4?	5	Not seen, but existence assumed.
Tc325	BK	1	A		✓		C1		Now known with back block C1.
Tc342	CE	4	A		✓	✓	WN3		Now known with "SA" serials.
Tc361A	DE	4	A	c Jul 83		✓	WL1	5	
Tc365A	DK	1	A	83		✓	WL1	5	
Tc405	OA	2	A	c Feb 84	✓	✓	OP2	9, 14	
Tc406	OB	2	C	84	✓		OP2	9	
Tc421	OC	2	A	27 Oct.85	✓		OP3	13	
Tc422	OC	2	A	86	✓		OP3	19	
Tc431	OL	2	A	Apr 86			OP4		
Tc441	ON	2	A	Apr 86	✓		OP5		
Tc491	B	Term	C			✓	Q		
Tc501	F	4	C	84		✓	Q	12	
Tc511	G	4	A	c Jan 84	✓	✓	Q	7	
Tc521	L	1	A	c Nov .83	✓	✓	Q	7	
Tc522	L	1	A	85	✓		Q	15	
Tc531	M	1	C	c Jan 84	✓	✓	Q	7	
Tc541	S	52	A	c 84	✓		S	16	
Tc551	T	52	A	2 Jan 85	✓		T	17	
Tc561	U	10	A	c 84	✓		Q	11	
Tc561A	U	10	A	c 83		✓	R	1	
Tc601	BE	4	A	84	✓		C4	8	
Tc611	BK	1	A	c Sep .83	✓	✓	C4	8	
Tc621	CE	4	A	84	✓		WN2	8	
Tc631	CK	1	A	c Mar 84	✓		WN2	8	
Tc632	CK	1	A	86	✓		WN2	18	
Tc641	DE	4	A	c Jan 84	✓		WL1	8	
Tc651	DK	1	A	c Jan 84	✓	✓	WL1	8	
Tc652	DK	1	A	86			WL1	18	

Travelcard Notes

1) These issues were printed by Booth, rather than Bemrose as previously. Frontal designs are identical to the Bemrose issues, but can be distinguished by virtue of having the 3-figure "sales point code" in ornate numerals and the serial numbers in smaller numerals.

"Countywide" issues by Booth carry Back block R, which is similar to the Bemrose Back block Q but in a more compressed layout.

Booth "design reference numbers" have been given an "A" suffix (e.g. Tc292A, Tc561A etc) to differentiate them from the equivalent Bemrose versions (Tc292, Tc561 etc.)

2) Hybrid cards, formed by converting obsolete Price Code E cards to G by blocking-out the "E" and the Route Code panel, and adding a "G" and the words "ALL ROUTES."

3) Probably during 1983, Students Term Tickets were retitled "Students Ten Week Tickets."

4) Four-week Child Countywide Travelcards were withdrawn from sale with effect from the 6 Sep 1981 fares reduction, but reinstated in July 1982. However, the disused Price Code F (previously used to denote a 4-week Adult card) was now reused for the above Child cards. Hitherto, Price Code J had been used.

5) Area Travelcards printed by Booth, rather than Bemrose as previously. Frontal designs are identical, but can be distinguished by virtue of having the 3-figure "sales point code" in ornate numerals and the serial numbers in smaller numerals.

Back blocks on Booth Area Travelcards appear to be identical to the Bemrose ones, and the same reference codes have been used (e.g. C4, WN3, WL1).

The frontal design reference numbers have been given an "A" suffix (e.g. Tc322A, Tc361A etc) to differentiate them from the equivalent Bemrose versions (Tc322, Tc361 etc.)

6) These Booth-printed cards omit the wording "ONE WEEK [OR FOUR WEEK] ADULT" and thus the fronts resemble the *first* version of Bemrose-printed Wolverhampton Travelcards, not the later version.

7) A slight redesign with 1) a panel drawn around "NOT VALID AFTER" and 2) "NOT TRANSFERABLE" squeezed in lower down.

8) The words "NOT TRANSFERABLE" added to the front of the card (as in Note 7 above.)

9) Latest validity time now shown as "23.29 hrs" instead of "22.15 hrs." "NOT TRANSFERABLE" added to the front of the card. Revised Back block (OP2), which shows the new validity time. Otherwise, the Back block is the same as OP1.

10) "13 WEEK ADULT" in smaller lettering than on Tc292.

11) Wording changed to "ADULT TEN WEEK TICKET."

12) "NOT TRANSFERABLE" added near bottom, but no panel around "NOT VALID AFTER" (See Note 7 above.)

13) Coventry Off Peak Travelcard. Yellow with purple printing, including back block.

14) Although not listed as a separate type, the wording to the right of "Two Week Adult" on some cards of Type Tc405, has a slightly different setting.

15) Another minor variety. The wording "For conditions see back" is in a noticeably larger type. This may well be found on other types of Travelcard.

16) A rather rare Travelcard, not often seen by members of the public. The top half of the card is grey with gold lettering and black serials, and the front has a shiny, laminated surface.

   These cards were issued only to WMPTE staff, and had the same validity as other Countywide Travelcards, except that they could not be used on Inter-City trains, only locals. As far as I am aware, these are the only Travelcards to have had this restriction. The card omits the wording "NOT TRANSFERABLE" on the front.

17) Similar in style to the previous type, Tc541, this is the "prestige" Annual Travelcard, sold to the public. The upper half is black with gold lettering, and serials are black on a white background panel. The front is shiny - not an easy surface on which to write one's name and address! A special leather wallet was provided for these.

18) WMPTE Sales Address on front of Travelcard changed from Whitmore Street to 16 Summer Lane, with consequent resetting of the type layout.

19) Slight redesign of upper section of Travelcard front. "SAT SUN" has been moved to the left, and "ALL DAY" is in larger lettering.

In the foregoing table of Travelcard types, two columns are headed "SA" and "SB." This refers to the position of the serial number in relation to the Price Code, and noticeably affects the appearance of the card. "SA" indicates that the serial number appears alongside the Price Code, whilst "SB" means that the serial number is below the level of the Price Code. Some cards appeared in both forms, but the foregoing table is by no means definitive - merely a guide, dependent on what is known to the writer.

Type Tc262 - salmon / dark blue

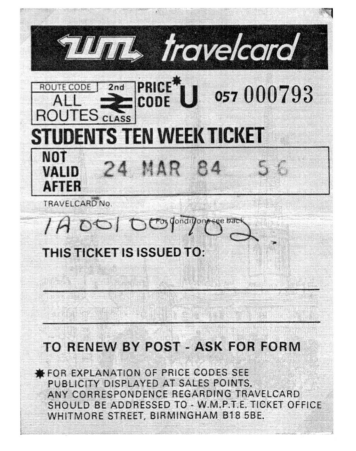

Tc281 - pink / dark blue

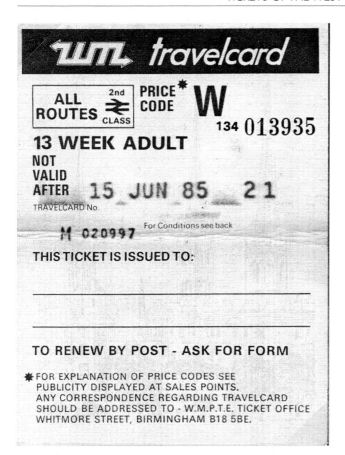

Type Tc293 - 13 Week Adult - lemon/dark blue

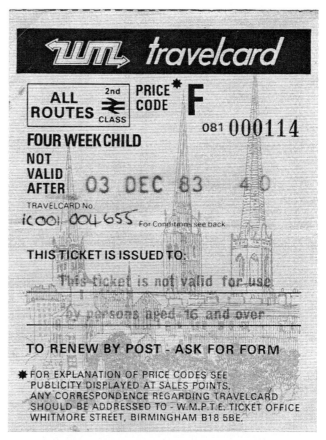

Tc296 - Four Week Child - salmon/dark blue

Type Tc365A - Walsall One Week Adult - buff/green

Type Tc406 - Two Week Off Peak Child - lemon/brown

Issued by the WMPTE in respect of Bus Services and British Railways Board in respect of Rail Services subject as may be appropriate to Road Traffic Acts. Public Service Vehicle Regulations Section 67 of the Transport Act 1962. British Railways Bye-Laws, Regulations, Conditions of Carriage of Passengers and their Luggage, Publications and Notices, and the WMPTE Travelcard Scheme. Insofar as the tickets relate to Rail Travel such tickets are issued by WMPTE as the British Railways Board's Agents and insofar as the tickets relate to Bus Travel such tickets are issued by the British Railways Board as the agents of the WMPTE.

Valid for bus and rail journeys without payment of a separate fare, as follows:

ON MONDAY TO FRIDAYS: 09.30 hours – 15.30 hours
18.00 hours – 23.29 hours

ON SATURDAYS AND SUNDAYS: start of service – 23.29 hours

1. Any WMPTE service bus within the West Midlands County.

2. Any Midland Red service bus operating on a service listed for this purpose in WMPTE publications within the West Midlands County.

3. Any British Rail train within the West Midlands County (2nd Class Only).

Where a pass holder boards a bus or train before scheduled departure time, the scheduled departure time is taken as the boarding time. Ordinary fare must be paid for any journey made outside ticket validity times.

Valid only for the person whose portrait is on the Travelcard. Valid only when accompanied by a Travelcard of the same number.

Does not give priority over other passengers. Lost tickets not replaced. Not transferable. Travelcard must be produced for examination on every journey. If not so produced, the ordinary fare must be paid, which is not refundable. Travelcard remains the property of the WMPTE and may be withdrawn by any of the above named operators if it is misused.

OP2 - back of Tc406

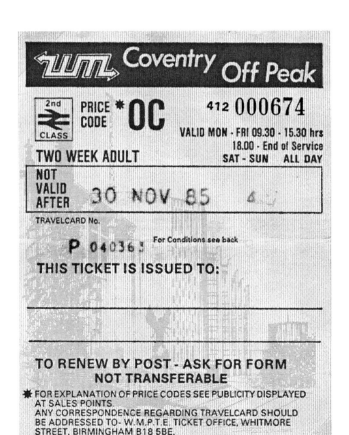

*Type Tc421 - Coventry Off-Peak Two Week Adult -
lemon/magenta*

Issued by the WMPTE in respect of Bus Services and British Railways Board in respect of Rail Services subject as may be appropriate to Road Traffic Acts Public Service Vehicle Regulations Section 67 of the Transport Act 1962. British Railways Bye-Laws, Regulations, Conditons of Carriage of Passengers and their Luggage, Publications and Notices, and the WMPTE Travelcard Scheme. Insofar as the tickets relate to Rail Travel such tickets are issued by WMPTE as the British Railways Board's Agents and insofar as the tickets relate to Bus Travel such tickets are issued by the British Railways Board as the agents of the WMPTE.

Valid for bus and rail journeys without payment of a separate fare, as follows:
ON MONDAY TO FRIDAYS 09.30 hours - 15.30 hours
18.00 hours - end of service
ON SATURDAYS AND SUNDAYS: All Day

Where a pass holder boards a bus or train before scheduled departure time, the scheduled departure time is taken as the boarding time. Ordinary fare must be paid for any journey made outside ticket validity times.

VALID FOR BUS TRAVEL, AS FOLLOWS
On any WMPTE service bus within the designated area except 159 and 900

On any Midland Red service bus operating on a service listed for this purpose in WMPTE publications within the designated area. Travecard is not valid on Midland Red buses leaving city/town centre terminal points between 15.30-18.00 hours Monday-Friday.

Valid only for the person whose portrait in on the Travelcard Photocard. Valid only when accompanied by a Travelcard Photocard of the same number. Does not give priority over other pasengers. Refunds not made. Lost tickets not replaced. Not Transferable. Travelcard must be produced for examination on every journey. If not so produced the ordinary fare must be paid which is not refundable. Travelcard remains the property of the WMPTE and may be withdrawn by any of the above named operators if it is misused.

Valid on British Rail between Coventry and Tile Hill only

OP3 - back of Tc421

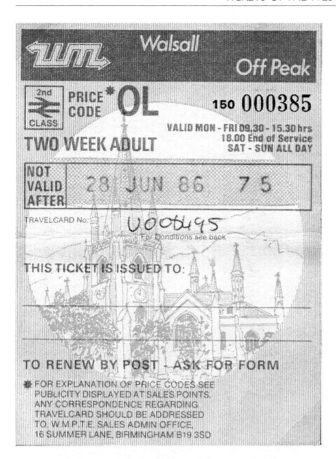

Type Tc431 - Walsall Off Peak Two Week Adult - lemon/pale blue

Issued by the WMPTE in respect of Bus Services and British Railways Board in respect of Rail Services subject as may be appropriate to Road Traffic Acts Public Service Vehicle Regulations Section 87 of the Transport Act 1962, British Railways Bye-Laws, Regulations, Conditions of Carriage of Passengers and their Luggage, Publications and Notices, and the WMPTE Travelcard Scheme. Insofar as the tickets relate to Rail Travel such tickets are issued by WMPTE as the British Railways Board's Agents and insofar as the tickets relate to Bus Travel such tickets are issued by the British Railways Board as the agents of the WMPTE.

Valid by bus journeys without payment of a separate fare, as follows:
ON MONDAY TO FRIDAYS 09.30 hours - 15.30 hours
18.00 hours - end of service
ON SATURDAYS AND SUNDAYS: All Day

Where a pass holder boards a bus before scheduled departure time, the scheduled departure time is taken as the boarding time. Ordinary fare must be paid for any journey made outside ticket validity times.

VALID FOR BUS TRAVEL, AS FOLLOWS
On any WMPTE service bus within the designated area.
On any Midland Red service bus operating on a service listed for this purpose in WMPTE publications within the designated area. Travelcard is not valid on Midland Red buses leaving city/town centre terminal points between 15.30-18.00 hours Monday-Friday.
Valid only for the person whose portrait is on the Travelcard Photocard. Valid only when accompanied by a Travelcard Photocard of the same number. Does not give priority over other passengers. Refunds not made. Lost tickets not replaced. Not Transferable. Travelcard must be produced for examination on every journey. If not so produced the ordinary fare must be paid which is not refundable. Travelcard remains the property of the WMPTE and may be withdrawn by any of the above named operators if it is misused.

Valid on British Rail between Walsall and Bescot only

OP4 - back of Tc431

Type Tc441 - Wolverhampton Off Peak Two Week Adult - lemon/pale salmon

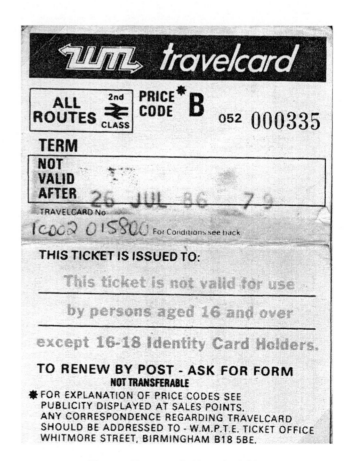

Tc491 - Term - pale blue/dark blue

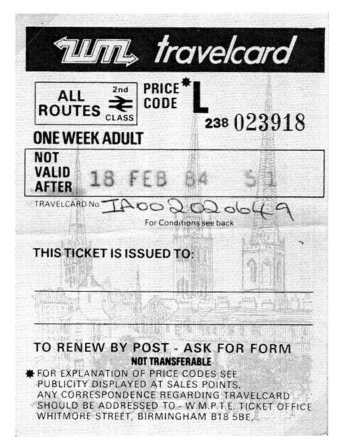

Type Tc521 - One Week Adult - buff/dark blue

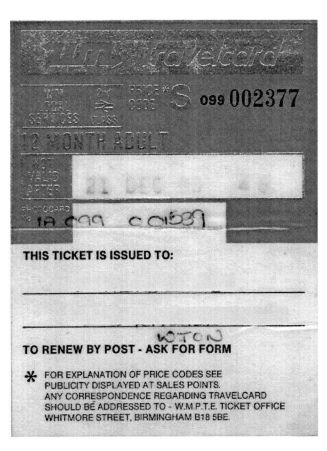

Type Tc541 - 12 Month Adult - grey/gold

Issued by the WMPTE in respect of Bus Services and British Railways Board in respect of Rail Services subject as may be appropriate to Road Traffic Acts, Public Service Vehicle Regulations Section 67 of the Transport Act 1962, British Railways Bye-Laws, Regulations, Conditions of Carriage of Passengers and their Luggage, Publications and Notices, and the WMPTE Travelcard Scheme. Insofar as the tickets relate to Rail Travel such tickets are issued by WMPTE as the British Railways Board's Agents and insofar as the tickets relate to Bus Travel such tickets are issued by the British Railways Board as the agents of the WMPTE.

Valid for journeys made on any WMPTE service bus in the West Midlands County except on any bus which leaves a terminal point at or after 23 30 hours and before 04 30 hours, without payment of separate fare. Valid on any Midland Red service bus operating on a service listed for this purpose in WMPTE publications. Travelcard is restricted on certain Midland Red buses leaving city/town centre terminal points between 15.30-18.00 hours Monday-Friday. Please see brochure.

Valid only for the person whose portrait is on the Photocard. Valid only when accompanied by a Photocard of the same number. Does not give priority over other passengers. Not transferable. Travelcard remains the property of the WMPTE and may be withdrawn by any of the participating operators if it is misused. This ticket to be produced on every journey. If not, ordinary fares must be paid which are not refundable.

Valid on British Rail Local Services (2ND CLASS ONLY) within the West Midlands County. Not Valid on Inter-City Services or Limited Stop Services on the Wolverhampton-Birmingham-Coventry rail route.

Back block S - back of Tc541

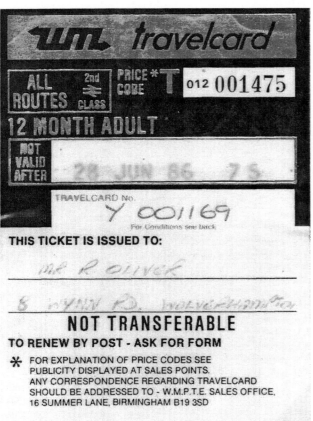

Issued by the WMPTE in respect of Bus Services and British Railways Board in respect of Rail Services subject as may be appropriate to Road Traffic Acts, Public Service Vehicle Regulations Section 67 of the Transport Act 1962, British Railways Bye-Laws, Regulations, Conditions of Carriage of Passengers and their Luggage, Publications and Notices and the WMPTE Travelcard Scheme. Insofar as the tickets relate to Rail Travel such tickets are issued by WMPTE as the British Railways Board Agents and insofar as the tickets relate to Bus Travel such tickets are issued by the British Railways Board as the agents of the WMPTE.

Valid for journeys made on any WMPTE service bus in the West Midlands County except on any bus which leaves a terminal point at or after 23.30 hours and before 04.30 hours, without payment of separate fare. Valid on any Midland Red service bus operating on a service listed for this purpose in WMPTE publications. Travelcard is restricted on certain Midland Red buses leaving city/town centre terminal points between 15.30-18.00 hours Monday-Friday. Please see brochure.

Valid only for the person whose portrait is on the Travelcard. Valid only when accompanied by a Travelcard of the same number. Does not give priority over other passengers. Not transferable. Travelcard remains the property of the WMPTE and may be withdrawn by any of the participating operators if it is misused. This ticket to be produced on every journey. If not, ordinary fares must be paid which are not refundable.

Valid on British Rail Services (2ND CLASS ONLY)
within the West Midlands County

Type Tc551 - 12 Month Adult - black/gold

Back block T - back of Tc551

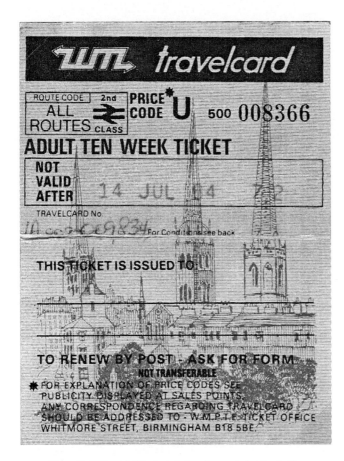

Type Tc561 - 10 Week Adult - deep pink/dark blue

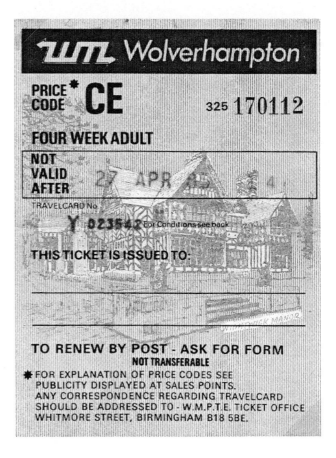

Tc621 - Wolverhampton Four Week Adult - salmon/dark blue

Fig 42 - Midland Railtourer

We end this chapter with three snippets of Travelcard information relating to an earlier period of time.

1) The following table (reproduced by courtesy of WMPTE) shows the number of Travelcards sold during the month of March, in each of the years 1975 - 1981.

'000s	Mar 1975	Mar 1976	Mar 1977	Mar 1978	Mar 1979	Mar 1980	Mar 1981
Bus only	55.2	65.0	69.1	72.9	65.5	68.9	-
Bus / Rail	-	10.4	18.3	23.5	42.2	55.9	116.0
Area / Short Distance	-	-	-	-	-	13.3	26.8
Total	55.2	75.4	87.4	96.4	107.7	138.1	142.8

Source: WMPTE

2) Early in 1983, the Passenger Transport Committee of the West Midlands County Council asked for a report on the possibility of introducing savings stamps which could be used for the purchase of Travelcards - like TV licence stamps etc. However, the Director General's report did not favour the idea, and no further action was taken.

3) The very first purchaser of a WMPTE Travelcard, in October 1972, was Mr Norman Taylor of Fordhouses, Wolverhampton. He received Travelcard No. 000001, and (at the time of writing this) still possessed the original card. Bus drivers used to call him "Number One." In 1988, Mr Taylor was invited by WMPTE's successor, West Midlands Travel, to open their new travel shop in Birmingham, and he also presented a Travelcard to the 25 millionth customer, the city's Lord Mayor.

This chapter could be subtitled "Scratching the Surface," because it makes no pretence of being a comprehensive story of concessionary travel for senior citizens on WMPTE buses. Taking the coward's way out, the writer intends to gloss over the 1969-1974 period fairly quickly! This is the period from the formation of WMPTE through to the setting up of the West Midlands County Council on 1st April 1974, during which time each of the former bus operating towns (and some of the other areas) had their own separate concessionary travel schemes for old age pensioners. Passes were issued by the councils themselves and did not - as far as I am aware - bear the PTE title. For this convenient reason, I can justify glossing over them!

If anyone is particularly interested in this rather minor backwater of ticket collecting, there is plenty of scope for research, though I imagine that it might be very difficult, at this distance in time, to unearth all the details. Each scheme was different, and permitted concessionary bus travel only within the relevant local authority's boundaries. Wolverhampton pensioners could not, for instance, travel to Walsall or Birmingham without payment of the full fare from the Borough boundary onwards.

In Wolverhampton, pensioners paid 1d and received (in Corporation Transport days) a special 1d yellow Ultimate ticket overprinted with a red "S" (presumably indicating Senior Citizen.) In PTE days, there was no special ticket, a current 1d ticket (1p after Decimalisation in 1971) being issued.

The 1967 Corporation timetable lays down that passholders could travel at the 1d fare between 9.30 and 16.30 on Mondays to Fridays, and all day Sunday. (These timings were later modified.) No concessionary travel was allowed on Saturdays, which contrasts sharply with the present day attitude of allowing unrestricted travel on Saturdays, and probably indicates a changing pattern of travel.

Most pensioners' travel schemes date from after the passing of the Travel Concessions Act of 1965, but some bus operators (including Birmingham) introduced schemes long before this date. Birmingham brought out a free travel for pensioners scheme in 1953 and quickly ran into trouble. A local ratepayer, Mr G. V. Prescot, challenged the legality of it in court, and won his case! The law was quickly modified in order to legalise similar schemes in other towns - but not Birmingham!

The TTS *Journal* for March 1970 reported that the PTE was "negotiating with all local authorities in the area to institute a comprehensive Aged Persons fares concession which would be available throughout the PTA [Passenger Transport Authority] area on all bus services." Some opposition had been encountered, principally from Midland Red who were concerned about loss of revenue when passes were used on their buses. The report went on to say that, in the meantime, "Birmingham Corporation have agreed to pay the PTE a sum of £350,000 to cover the cost of free travel in the Birmingham area only, from 1st April 1970 to 31st March 1971. All existing Birmingham Corporation passes will be called in, and new passes, with validity extended to include Sundays, will be issued from 1st April 1970."

These early hopes for a unified scheme did not reach fruition for another 4 years, by which time most of the Midland Red services in the West Midlands area had been taken over by the PTE.

However, a useful agreement was reached with Midland Red and certain local authorities, whereby the latter could buy passes for issuing to their pensioners, allowing half fare travel (up to a stipulated maximum) during off peak hours. These were known as "blue and white" passes, and were used by a number of local authorities in the PTE area. Passholders could use them on both the WMPTE and Midland Red buses. The 1973 WMPTE Wolverhampton timetable states: "Persons

in possession of a Blue and White pass, headed Old Person's Travel Pass (Child's Fare) issued by Local Authorities may travel at childrens' fare scales from 09.30 to 15.30 and 18.30 to 21.30 Monday to Friday and Sunday until 21.30, where the adult fare is not more than 14p."

Let's skip hastily over the plethora of different passes and different regulations, and pick up the story in 1974. To their credit, the new West Midlands County Council lost no time in bringing in a unified scheme whereby pensioners could travel free of charge anywhere in the County.

> *"From 1st April 1974,"* said the publicity leaflet, *"men aged 65 and over and women aged 60 and over resident in the West Midlands County may travel FREE within the County with their existing passes provided the bus is boarded between the following times:*
> *MONDAYS TO FRIDAYS*
> *9.30am and 3.30pm : 6.00pm and 9.30pm.*
> *SATURDAYS 9.30am and 3.30pm.*
> *SUNDAYS Start of service and 9.30pm*
> *Passes will be valid on ALL buses within the County."*

The latter sentence implied that passes could not only be used on WMPTE buses, but also on Midland Red and on certain sections of route operated by the moribund (and sadly missed) independent, Harper Bros. of Heath Hayes who were taken over by Midland Red in 1974.

This new scheme, of course, replaced all existing ones within the WM County, but neighbouring local authorities continued to administer separate schemes and issue their own passes. Here again, there is much scope for research, if the subject appeals to anybody. I think it is true to say that these "Shire Passes" confer reduced fares rather than free travel. The 1974 West Midlands scheme did not immediately apply to Coventry, whose bus system had only just been taken over by the PTE.

As the old passes became due for renewal, they were replaced by new ones carrying the WMPTE title, but these were still obtainable from the local council offices (not PTE offices) and had to be renewed every 12 months. Two versions are illustrated below, and there may well have been other types. (Figs 43 and 44).

The next milestone was 5th February 1979, when the use of pensioners' passes was extended to the local rail network for the first time. Passes had to be stamped at railway stations before they could be used on trains. Unlike Travelcards, which since 1975 have been valid on all trains within the County, pensioners' passes were (until 1990) restricted to local stopping trains (i.e. not Inter City services.) Some pensioners "tried it on" and travelled on Inter City trains - either through genuine ignorance of the rules or in the hope of getting away with it! I heard tell of one old lady who had used her pass to travel to Bournemouth!!

Also from early 1979, the card passes were gradually replaced (as they became due for renewal) by plastic "data cards" resembling credit cards (Fig 45). The illustration is taken from the cover of the publicity leaflet which proclaimed *"Here's something that will really last!"*

The passes carried a photograph of the holder which the earlier cardboard ones had not. They were intended to last indefinitely, thus cutting out the cost and inconvenience of the annual renewal. By this time, the original validity timings had been improved, and were now:

Mondays to Fridays - 9.30am to 3.30pm, 6.00pm - 10.15pm.
Saturdays, Sundays and Bank Holidays - Start of service to 10.15pm.

Also, since 1978, passes were accepted (within the WM County) on the expanding route network of Mid-Warwickshire Motors Ltd., an independent company operating mainly in the Solihull / Coventry region.

In more recent years, the frontal design of the plastic card passes was slightly modified, and a slightly different version is shown in Fig 46. The illustration is taken from a PTE leaflet.

On 28th December 1983, the time limits were again improved, this time quite dramatically:

Mondays to Fridays - 9.30am to 11.29pm.
Saturdays, Sundays and Bank Holidays
  - Start of service to 11.29pm.

With the threat of Deregulation, and all the problems which it posed for both bus operators and passengers, many people felt that pensioners passes were in danger of being abolished, and the matter became a subject for emotive political argument. However in April 1986, after the abolition of the West Midlands County Council, the seven District Councils issued a joint statement to the effect that the pensioners free travel scheme would be continued.

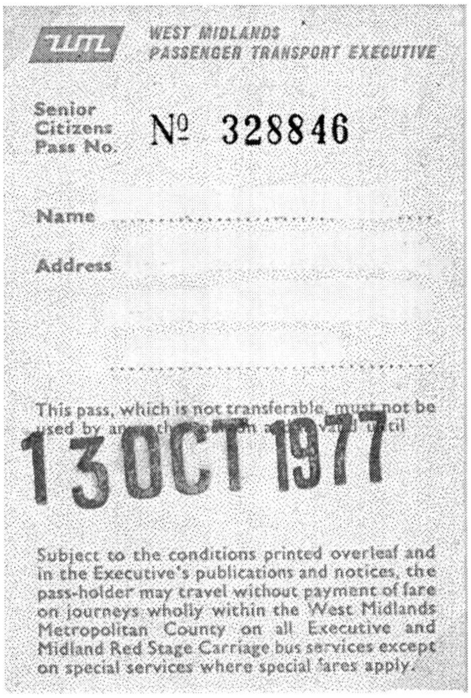

Fig 43

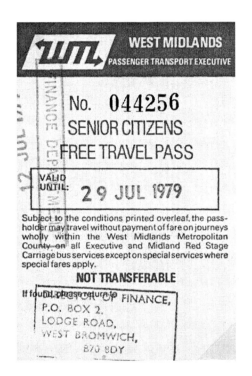

Fig 44

Fig 45

Fig 46

5   Scholars Passes

Scratching the surface again! Here is another very complicated subject which isn't easy to unravel, but I have managed to piece together enough information to present a general picture. Forgive me if I appear to gloss over some of the details rather quickly - the full information just isn't available without access to official records, and perhaps not even then. Consequently, this chapter doesn't claim to be a complete history of concessionary travel for school children or students in the WMPTE area, and there must be many passes which are not illustrated or described. In this chapter we are dealing with five basic types of ticket, pass, permit, call them what you like. These are:

1) Free Travel Passes, issued to Children living more than the specified distance from school / college.

2) Half Fare Passes, issued to Children living less than the specified distance from school / college, and entitling them to travel at child's fare. A travel ticket would have to be purchased from the driver / conductor in the normal way.

3) Weekly Prepaids. (Walsall District issues.)

4) Term Tickets. Prepaid half fare passes.

5) Scholars Tickets. i.e. the type introduced in 1982, which served the purpose of either 1) or 4) above, as appropriate.

To confuse matters even further, the shape, style and (moreover) title of the various passes varied considerably over the years, and different divisions or districts of the PTE used different styles. The basic conditions relating to scholars concessionary travel were as follows:

1) Teenagers up to (but not including) the age of 16 could travel at child's fare. Prior to 13th August 1978, the age limit was 15.

2) Teenagers aged 16-18 and in full time education could (until the Autumn term of 1981) travel at child's fare provided they had the necessary pass. These were valid until the end of the academic year in which the 18th birthday fell. From September 1981, they had to have a Term Ticket, or Scholar's Ticket, as described later.

3) School children and students in the foregoing categories were entitled to free travel between home and school or college, if the distance was more than 3 miles by the shortest route. They had to have a free travel pass, obtainable from their Local Education Authority.

In all the above cases, passes were only valid for journeys to / from school or college, or in connection with the school curriculum. They could not be used for leisure travel or at weekends.

So much for the conditions. What about the actual tickets? Let's deal first with:

Free Travel Passes

These came in numerous different guises. Various types are illustrated further on (Figs 52-61) but no doubt there were others. Printing was mainly blue in every case except Fig 56 which had black printing and a red "F" overprint.

From 1978 to 1982, free passes took the form of a white plastic "data card" with red title panel and red printing (Figs 62 and 63). Similar cards were provided for prepaid half fare use, on a termly basis, for children not entitled to free travel. This avoided the need to find change each day. Prices were "tailored" according to the daily fare applicable. To some extent, these were the forerunner of

the Scholars Tickets introduced in 1982.

Whereas free passes were obtainable from the Local Education Authorities, the prepaid passes were only available from PTE Travel Centres.

Now we can move on to:-

Half Fare Passes

These were not travel tickets in their own right, but constituted evidence that the holder was entitled to travel at Child's fare, and had to be produced for inspection upon request. A normal ticket would have to be purchased for each journey.

Entitled "Students Half Fare Travel Permit," the specimen in Figs 65 and 66 gives no clue as to its date, but is probably early 1970's. Colour is blue with a green flash. A later version is shown in Figs 67 and 68. The title has changed to "Scholars Identity Card," and the pass is on stiff card with orange heading and diagonal stripe. Unlike previous versions, this card refers to rail validity between specified points.

From the Autumn Term of 1978 these were replaced by a white plastic "data card" with orange heading and stripe. Two varieties are illustrated in this chapter (Figs 69 to 71), the second one apparently being restricted to rail travel.

These plastic passes were discontinued in July 1981, after 3 academic years. Thereafter, no half fare passes were issued, and (from September 1981) child travel tickets ceased to be available for students aged 16-18. They had to have a Term Ticket (later known as Scholars Tickets) as described shortly.

Prepaid Weekly Tickets (Walsall District)

Illustrated in Figs 72-76, these white card tickets were only used in Walsall District and were closely based on the old Walsall Corporation design used prior to the PTE taking over.

The specified limits of travel were entered on each ticket, and there were cancellation spaces for the conductor to punch when each journey was made. Tickets were pre-priced according to the normal fare from home to school.

Some tickets had red printing and some black. It seems that the red ones were for use when two buses were needed to complete a journey, and the black-printed ones were for use when only one bus was needed.

I don't know how many values existed - no doubt there were many more than those listed here. The 2/6d and 3/2d versions obviously date back to the 1969/70 period and show "Northern Division" in the title. This was an early rendering before things settled down and they standardised on "North Division." The 2/6d ticket bears the signature of Mr S. Jobling, who was the last General Manager of West Bromwich Corporation Transport and the first Operations Manager of WMPTE North(ern) Division. All the other tickets listed here show Mr K. R. Sutton's name. Known issues are:-

Red Printing	_Black Printing_
2/6d, 3/2d, 23p,	13p, 16p, 19p,
30p, 38p, 45p.	32p, 45p.

Term Tickets

In 1981/2, the whole system was changed. A yellow publicity leaflet gave details of a £3.50 Term Ticket on sale from the Autumn Term of 1981. This was available to school children under 16 and full time students aged 16-18. As mentioned earlier, students in the latter category could no longer buy childs fare tickets from the bus driver. Term Tickets gave unlimited travel (without further payment) between home and school or college, plus additional journeys in connection with the curriculum.

They could be purchased from PTE Travel Centres and Travelcard agents, plus certain schools.

Students in the 16-18 age group had to have a special identity card (Fig 47) which was carried in a free wallet together with the Term Ticket. Identity cards had to be signed by the Head Teacher or Principal. The illustrated specimen had red printing and black serials.

The remarkably low price of these Term Tickets was linked to the PTE's "cheap fares" scheme introduced on 6th September 1981. Fares were drastically reduced, and children under 16 were allowed to make any journey for a mere 2p! This led to many complaints about increased nuisance on the buses, and allegations that some parents were giving their children a handful of 2p coins and telling them to go out and play on the buses!

Following legal advice, the cheap fares policy was abandoned in March 1982, and fares were substantially increased again. The 2p childs fare was abolished - much to the relief of many older people!

Just to confuse the issue, there was an earlier ticket with a similar title, known as the Students Term Ticket and introduced in 1979. This was a member of the vast and unbelievably complicated Travelcard family. At an uncertain date (c. 1983) these were renamed Students Ten Week Tickets, and in about 1984 were again renamed Adult Ten Week Travelcards. Price Code U was used in each case. These Travelcards should not be confused with the Term Tickets of 1981, as described in this chapter.

Scholars Tickets

A new range of prepaid tickets for school children and students - known as Scholars Tickets - was introduced on 14th April 1982, and the existing Term Tickets were incorporated into the range. Conditions were the same as for Term Tickets.

Initially, tickets for one week (£2), 4 weeks (£6.50) or a full term (£18) were advertised, but other varieties were added later. A list of all known types is included further on.It will be noted that the price of a termly ticket had rocketed from £3.50 to £18 as a result of the abolition of the cheap fares scheme!

Even with Scholars Tickets, not all information is available. Originally, tickets were printed by Booth, with (in most cases) the Price Code and lettering in black, title panel and the word "scholars" in red, and with distinctive ornate numerals used for the sales point code (i.e. the 3-digit code to the left of the serial number.)

Later, tickets were printed by Bemrose, whom the PTE had patronised for many years, particularly in respect of Travelcards. Bemrose Scholars Tickets were quite different from Booth issues, with a smaller, heavier looking Price Code, and with most of the lettering (including the Price Code) in red instead of black. Also, the colour of the security background sometimes differed between the two printers. I am not certain if all Price Code

varieties were produced by both printers, but for the purpose of the Checklist it is assumed that they were. For instance, I am doubtful if Booth printed any "Scholar Plus" (SP) tickets. This was a later addition to the range and appears to have been the first Bemrose issue.

In the illustrations, at the end of this chapter, I have used a letter H to indicate Booth issues, and a letter E for Bemrose. Obviously I could not use B for both of them, so I have used the last letter of each name Thus, SA (E) indicates a full academic year Scholars Ticket printed by Bemrose.

"*If you are a Warwickshire or Staffordshire Scholar travelling to school or college within these counties or across the West Midlands County Boundary,*" said the green publicity leaflet issued to promote Scholars Tickets, "*you may obtain a special identity card from WMPTE Travel Centres. Production of this card for school or college journeys on WMPTE services will secure child fare.*" This (presumably) refers to Price Code SS, ST and SU Scholars Tickets, two of which are illustrated at the very end of this chapter.

Children or students who qualified for free travel could obtain a free Scholars Ticket from their Local Education Authority. Usually this would be a Price Code SA ticket, valid for a full school year. By purchasing a "Scholar Plus" ticket (SP), they could "convert" their SA card into a Travelcard, which they could use outside school hours, at weekends, and during school holidays - but not the long summer holiday! In appearance, the SP was rather unusual by virtue of having blue lettering and a large white cross.

Those who were not entitled to free travel could purchase Scholars Tickets from WMPTE Travel Centres or agents, at the prices quoted in the following list.

With the approach of Deregulation, Scholars Tickets were withdrawn from sale after the end of the 1985/6 academic year, and would-be purchasers were referred to the small range of Young Persons Travelcards. However, LEAs continued to issue Scholars Tickets to those who qualified for free travel.

The following table is incomplete in various respects, but I'm working on the principle that half a loaf is better than no bread … ! For a start, the Printers columns are incomplete. The information is based solely on examples known to the writer. Background colours are sometimes difficult to assess accurately, and in some cases vary between the two printers. These colours should be used only as a guide, and not taken as definitive.

Dates of Introduction are uncertain in many cases. With regard to the price increases of March 1985 and April 1986, the new prices applied to tickets purchased in advance from 27th March 1985 and 2nd April 1986 respectively.

Table of Scholars Tickets 1982 - 1986

Price Code	Description	Booth	Bemrose	Colour	Date introduced	Initial price	Price increases 31 Mar 1985	6 Apr 1986	Notes
SA	Academic Year	*	*	yellow	Sep 83	£54.00	£58.50	£67.50	1
SB	Two Terms	*		yellow		£36.00	£39.00		
SC	One Term	*		blue	14 Apr 82	£18.00	£19.50	£22.50	
SD	Duplicate	*		yellow		£4.00	£4.00		2
SE	Two Weeks			yellow		£4.00	£4.20		
SG	Four Weeks	*	*	pink	14 Apr 82	£6.50	£7.00	£8.00	
SL	One Week	*	*	brown	14 Apr 82	£2.00	£2.10	£2.40	
SP	Scholar Plus (One Year)		*	yellow	Sep 83	£11.00	£11.50	£13.00	3
SS	Academic Year	*		cream with brown text					4
ST	Half Term	*		cream with brown text					4
SU	Duplicate			cream with brown text					2, 4

Notes to table of Scholars Tickets:

1) This was the type normally issued to people who qualified for free travel, but could also be purchased by those who did not.
2) Types SD and SU were issued to replace lost tickets.
3) Scholar Plus tickets were used to convert a Type SA into a Travelcard, for use in the evenings and at weekends, etc. Since the SA would expire at the end of the Summer Term, these tickets were not available during the long summer holidays.
4) These cards were issued to children or students living in Staffordshire or Warwickshire.

Photocard

From September 1981, students aged 16-18 had to carry an identity card with their Term Ticket or (later) Scholars Ticket. This is shown in Fig 47 below.

However, *"from the start of the Autumn Term"* (1983), said a blue publicity leaflet which showed Wumpty wearing a mortar board instead of his driver's cap, *"you will need to carry a Photocard along with your Scholars Ticket when using the bus or train."* This referred both to students aged 16-18 and also children under 16.

Photocards were white plastic cards measuring about 66 cm x 54 cm, and could be obtained by taking a passport size colour photo (plus 35p) to a WMPTE Travel Centre. Alternatively, one could (in most cases) have a photograph taken at the Travel Centre for 50p. The photo would then be transferred onto the plastic card. Holders of an existing Child Travelcard identity card could use this instead of buying a Photocard. New applicants for Child Travelcards also had to have a Photocard to go with it.

Child Photocards (under 16) had light blue printing, (Fig 48), whereas the colour on the 16-18 age group cards was changed at the beginning of each academic year. The 1984/5 card illustrated in Fig 49 had green printing. There was also an Adult Photocard for use with Travelcards, and these had dark blue printing.

Coventry Project Ticket, 1984

Squeezing in at the tail end of this chapter is this special ticket issued by WMPTE (East Division) during the school summer term of 1984. Coventry Education Department asked the PTE to provide travel passes for use by school children taking part in a Department of Education & Science special project. This was a day release scheme, with different schools attending on different days of the week. WMPTE sold the tickets in bulk to the Education Department, who then issued them to the relevant pupils.

Tickets were valid for free travel on the specified day of the week, for one return journey made prior to 6 p.m. They could be used on all WMPTE services in Coventry except the 159 (Birmingham) route. The illustrated specimen (Figs 50 and 51) shows "Wednesday," but there were undoubtedly tickets for the other weekdays too.

My thanks to West Midlands Travel Ltd. (Coventry Office) for kindly assisting with the details concerning these tickets.

Fig 47

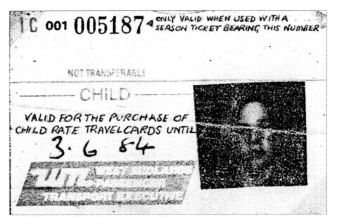

Fig 48

Fig 49

Fig 50

Fig 51 - reverse of Fig 50

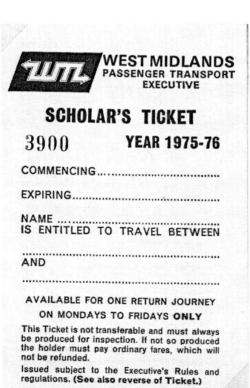

WEST MIDLANDS
PASSENGER TRANSPORT EXECUTIVE

SCHOLARS FREE TRAVEL PERMIT No. 1558

EXPIRY DATE

FREE TRAVEL AVAILABLE

From ....

....

To ....

....

Via ....

Validity:

Monday to Friday, for one journey in each direction, daily, to and from school only, for school purposes.

NOT Valid:

1. During School Holidays.
2. During Lunchtimes.
3. If bus is boarded after 1800.

NOT TRANSFERABLE

For Conditions of Issue— See over

Fig 52

CONDITIONS OF ISSUE

1. This Permit is issued subject to the Executive's Rules and Regulations. It is not transferable and must be produced for inspection on all occasions.

2. This Permit does not entitle the holder to any priorities over other passengers.

3. This Permit will be rendered invalid if altered, mutilated or defaced.

4. The Executive will not accept any liability or responsibility for delays or any consequential damages arising from any cause whatsoever.

5. If this Permit is lost the circumstances must be reported immediately to the Education Authority. Replacement will be made only in exceptional circumstances and a charge (minimum 50p) will be made.

6. On expiry this Permit must be returned to any WMPTE office.

7. This Permit is only valid if signed in space provided below. Signature thereof implies acceptance of these conditions.

Scholar's Signature ....

Full Name ....
(Block Letters)

Address ....
(Block Letters)

....

Fig 53 - reverse of Fig 52

WEST MIDLANDS
PASSENGER TRANSPORT
EXECUTIVE

SCHOLAR'S TICKET

3900   YEAR 1975-76

COMMENCING................................

EXPIRING................................

NAME ....
IS ENTITLED TO TRAVEL BETWEEN

....
AND

....

AVAILABLE FOR ONE RETURN JOURNEY
ON MONDAYS TO FRIDAYS **ONLY**

This Ticket is not transferable and must always be produced for inspection. If not so produced the holder must pay ordinary fares, which will not be refunded.

Issued subject to the Executive's Rules and regulations. (See also reverse of Ticket.)

Fig 54

CONDITIONS of ISSUE

1. If this Ticket is lost or damaged a replacement can be obtained from the issuing authority upon payment of the appropriate fee.

2. This Ticket will be rendered invalid if altered, mutilated or defaced.

3. This Ticket does not entitle the holder to any priorities over other passengers.

4. This Ticket must be surrendered immediately after the last day of expiry.

5. This Ticket may be used on journeys to and from school only.

6. The Executive will not accept any liability or responsibility for delays or any consequential damages arising from any cause whatsoever.

7. In cases of abuse the Executive hold the right to withdraw the pass.

Holder's Signature................................

Address ....

....

WEST MIDLANDS
PASSENGER TRANSPORT EXECUTIVE
16, SUMMER LANE,
BIRMINGHAM B19 3SD

Fig 55 - reverse of Fig 54

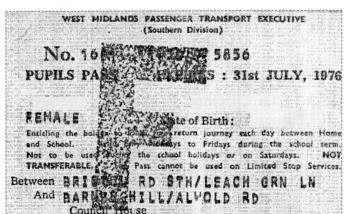

WEST MIDLANDS PASSENGER TRANSPORT EXECUTIVE
(Southern Division)

No. 16 5856
PUPILS PA S : 31st JULY, 1976

FEMALE te of Birth:
Entitling the holder to return journey each day between Home
and School. ys to Fridays during the school term.
Not to be used the school holidays or on Saturdays. NOT
TRANSFERABLE. Pass cannot be used on Limited Stop Services.
Between BRIG RD STH/LEACH GRN LN
And BARN HILL/ALWOLD RD
Council House
Birmingham   F. G. SIMONS
B3 3HL   Operations Manager

Fig 56

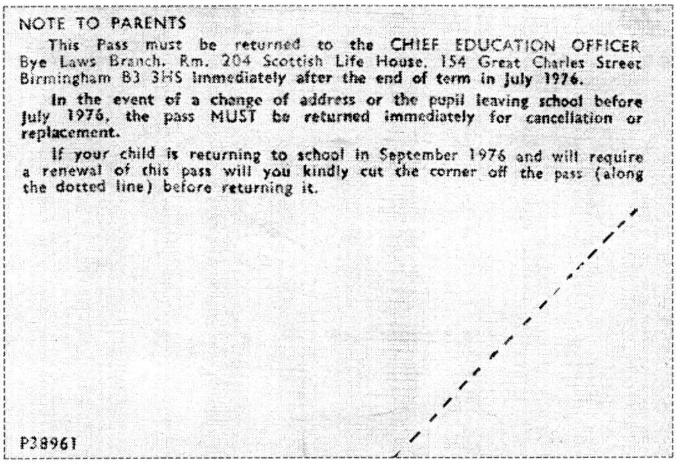

Fig 57 - reverse of Fig 56

NOTE TO PARENTS
This Pass must be returned to the CHIEF EDUCATION OFFICER
Bye Laws Branch, Rm. 204 Scottish Life House, 154 Great Charles Street
Birmingham B3 3HS immediately after the end of term in July 1976.
In the event of a change of address or the pupil leaving school before
July 1976, the pass MUST be returned immediately for cancellation or
replacement.
If your child is returning to school in September 1976 and will require
a renewal of this pass will you kindly cut the corner off the pass (along
the dotted line) before returning it.

P38961

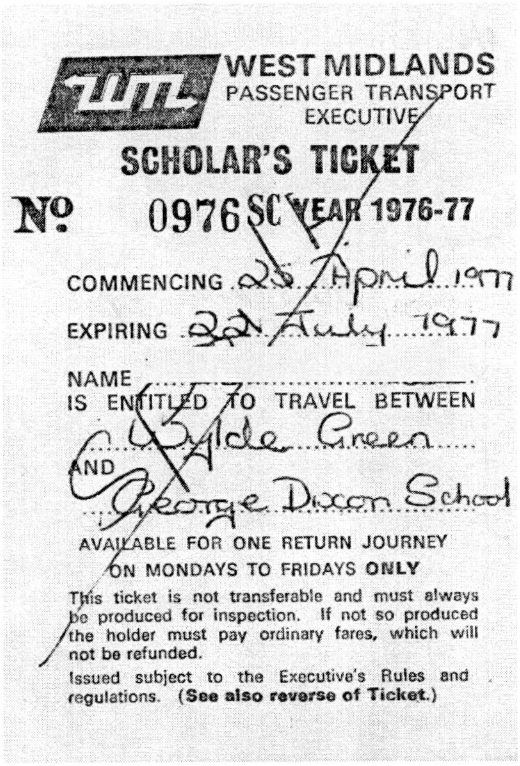

WEST MIDLANDS PASSENGER TRANSPORT EXECUTIVE

SCHOLAR'S TICKET

No. 0976 SC YEAR 1976-77

COMMENCING 25 April 1977

EXPIRING 22 July 1977

NAME
IS ENTITLED TO TRAVEL BETWEEN
Wylde Green
AND
George Dixon School

AVAILABLE FOR ONE RETURN JOURNEY
ON MONDAYS TO FRIDAYS ONLY

This ticket is not transferable and must always
be produced for inspection. If not so produced
the holder must pay ordinary fares, which will
not be refunded.

Issued subject to the Executive's Rules and
regulations. **(See also reverse of Ticket.)**

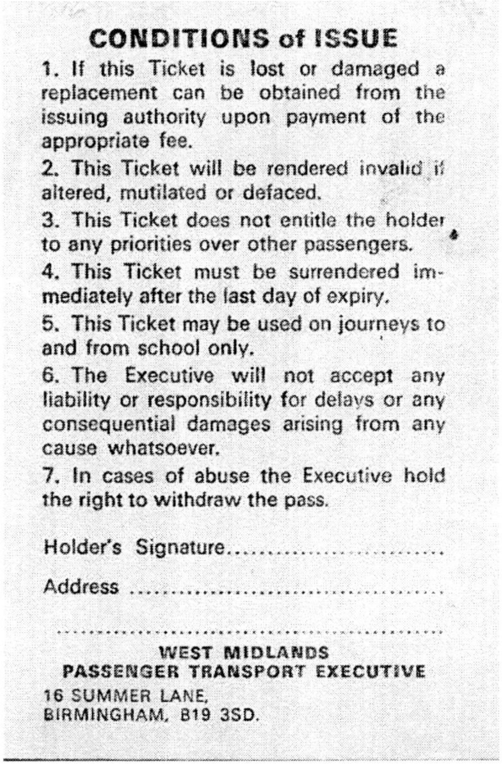

CONDITIONS of ISSUE

1. If this Ticket is lost or damaged a
replacement can be obtained from the
issuing authority upon payment of the
appropriate fee.
2. This Ticket will be rendered invalid if
altered, mutilated or defaced.
3. This Ticket does not entitle the holder
to any priorities over other passengers.
4. This Ticket must be surrendered immediately after the last day of expiry.
5. This Ticket may be used on journeys to
and from school only.
6. The Executive will not accept any
liability or responsibility for delays or any
consequential damages arising from any
cause whatsoever.
7. In cases of abuse the Executive hold
the right to withdraw the pass.

Holder's Signature.............................

Address ....

....

WEST MIDLANDS
PASSENGER TRANSPORT EXECUTIVE
16 SUMMER LANE,
BIRMINGHAM, B19 3SD.

Fig 58   *Fig 59 - reverse of Fig 58*

WEST MIDLANDS
PASSENGER TRANSPORT EXECUTIVE

No. 017073
SCHOLARS FREE
TRAVEL TICKET

VALID
UNTIL:

THE HOLDER IS
ENTITLED TO TRAVEL BETWEEN

AND

VIA

NOT TRANSFERABLE

**VALID FOR ONE RETURN JOURNEY
BETWEEN THE ABOVE POINTS
ONLY, MONDAY TO FRIDAY
NOT VALID IF BUS IS BOARDED
AFTER 18.00**

For Conditions of Issue – See over

Fig 60

CONDITIONS OF ISSUE

1. Issued subject to the published terms and conditions relating to the Executive's services and facilities which are available for inspection at divisional offices at 16 Summer Lane, Birmingham, St. Paul's Street Walsall, and Harnall Lane East, Coventry.
2. This ticket must be produced for inspection. If not so produced ordinary fares must be paid which will not be refunded.
3. If this ticket is lost or damaged a replacement may be obtained from the issuing authority upon payment of the appropriate fee.
4. This ticket will be rendered invalid if altered, mutilated or defaced.
5. This ticket does not entitle the holder to any priorities over other passengers.
6. This ticket must be surrendered immediately after the last day of expiry.
7. The Executive will not accept any liability or responsibility for delays or any consequential damages arising from any cause whatsoever.
8. In cases of abuse the Executive hold the right to withdraw the pass.

This permit is only valid if signed below. Signing thereof implies acceptance of these conditions.

Holder's Signature ....

Address ....

....

Fig 61 - reverse of Fig 60

WEST MIDLANDS
PASSENGER TRANSPORT EXECUTIVE

SCHOLARS TRAVEL PASS

Valid on British Rail between:

Valid on bus between: Valid Until: 18 JUL 80

and   BURTON RD
via   COALWAY RD/PENN RD
      No. G8409 1133 10884

Name

Fig 62

CONDITIONS OF ISSUE

1. Issued subject to the Regulations and Conditions in the Publications and Notices of the British Railways Board and the Published Terms and Conditions relating to the Executive and Midland Red's services and Facilities which are available for inspection at the respective companies' offices.
2. The holder is entitled to make one return journey, Monday to Friday during school terms between the points specified over (2nd Class only on Rail) using only those services indicated. Not valid after 22.15 hours.
3. This pass must be produced for inspection. If not so produced ordinary fares must be paid which will not be refunded.
4. This pass will be rendered invalid if altered, mutilated or defaced.
5. In cases of misuse, officials of the operator concerned have the right to withdraw the pass.
6. This pass does not entitle the holder to any priorities over other passengers.
7. The Executive and/or British Rail will not accept any liability or responsibility for delays or any consequential damages arising from any cause whatsoever.
8. This card must be surrendered immediately after the day of expiry.
9. If this card is lost or damaged a replacement can be obtained from the issuing authority upon payment of the appropriate fee.

NOT TRANSFERABLE

Fig 63 - reverse of Fig 62

WEST MIDLANDS PASSENGER TRANSPORT EXECUTIVE

is No. 484

The undermentioned is under ~~14~~ years of age and is entitled to travel at Children's Fares at any time.

Name ....

Address ....

EXPIRES

-9 JUN 1972

This Card must be produced on demand. It must be returned to the Office of Issue immediately after the above date.

NOT TRANSFERABLE

Fig 64

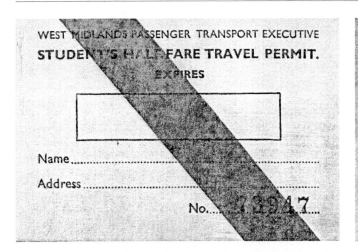

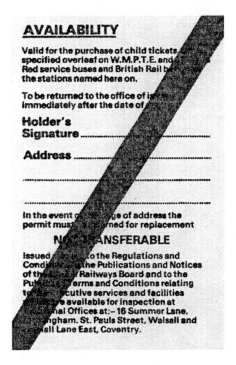

Fig 65

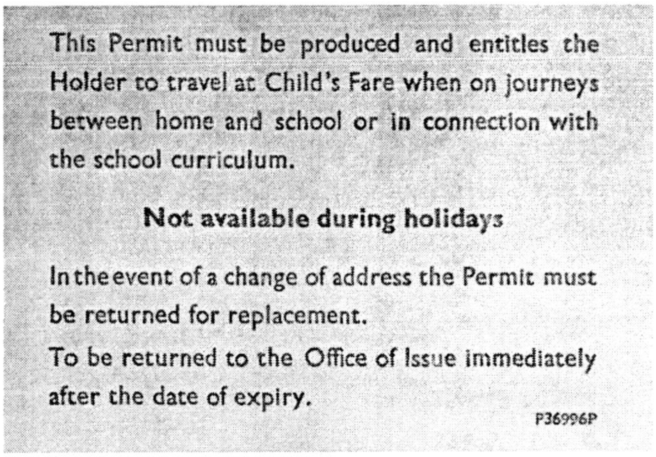

Fig 66 - reverse of Fig 65

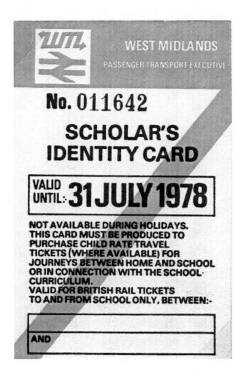

Fig 67

Fig 68 - reverse of Fig 67

Fig 69

Fig 70

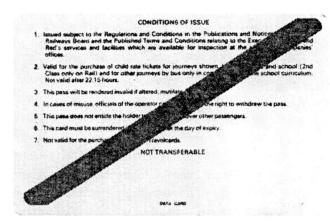

Fig 71 - reverse of Figs 69 and 70

A **4629**

WEST MIDLANDS PASSENGER TRANSPORT
EXECUTIVE (NORTHERN DIVISION)
(WALSALL DISTRICT)

SCHOLAR'S WEEKLY SEASON TICKET
FARE 2/6

This Ticket entitles the Holder to make
one return journey each day
TO AND FROM SCHOOL ONLY

NOT TRANSFERABLE

Name

- -

This Ticket is to be given up to Conductor
on expiry.

Issued subject to
Bye-Laws and Regulations.

S. JOBLING,
Operations Manager.

TRANSPORT OFFICES,
WALSALL.

Fig 72

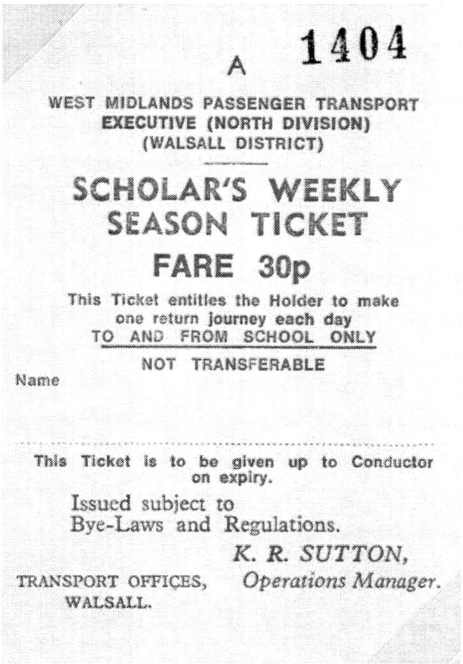

A **1404**

WEST MIDLANDS PASSENGER TRANSPORT
EXECUTIVE (NORTH DIVISION)
(WALSALL DISTRICT)

SCHOLAR'S WEEKLY SEASON TICKET
FARE 30p

This Ticket entitles the Holder to make
one return journey each day
TO AND FROM SCHOOL ONLY

NOT TRANSFERABLE

Name

- -

This Ticket is to be given up to Conductor
on expiry.

Issued subject to
Bye-Laws and Regulations.

K. R. SUTTON,
Operations Manager.

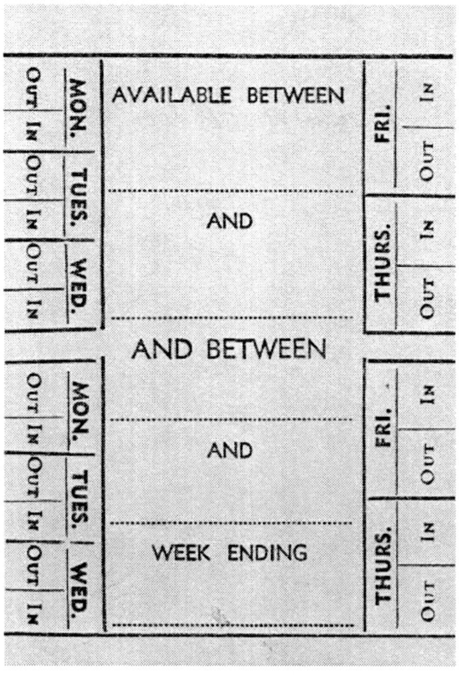

TRANSPORT OFFICES,
WALSALL.

Fig 73

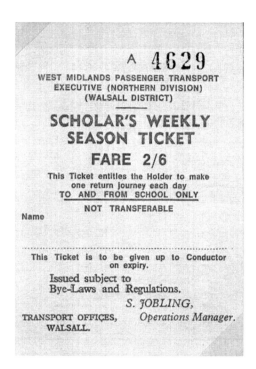

Fig 74 - reverse of Figs 72 and 73

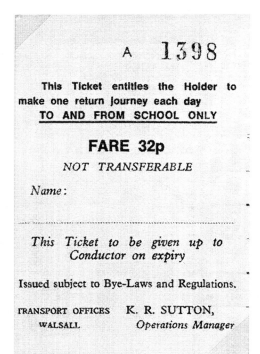

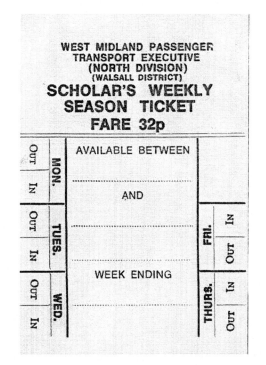

Fig 75

Fig 76 - reverse of Fig 75

SA (H)

reverse

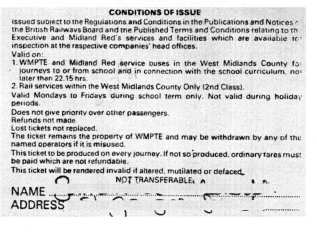

SA (E)

reverse

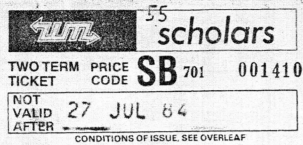

55

scholars

TWO TERM TICKET — PRICE CODE **SB** 701 — 001410

NOT VALID AFTER — 27 JUL 84

CONDITIONS OF ISSUE, SEE OVERLEAF

2nd CLASS

NOT AVAILABLE FOR USE ON SATURDAYS AND SUNDAYS

◄◄ Enter Identity Card Number (16-18 Age Group Only)

SB (H)

CONDITIONS OF ISSUE

Issued subject to the Regulations and Conditions in the Publications and Notices of the British Railways Board and the Published Terms and Conditions relating to the Executive and Midland Red's services and facilities which are available for inspection at the respective companies' head offices.

Valid on:
1. WMPTE and Midland Red service buses in the West Midlands County for journeys to or from school and in connection with the school curriculum, not later than 22.15 hrs.
2. Rail services within the West Midlands County Only (2nd Class).

Valid Mondays to Fridays during school term only. Not valid during holiday periods.

Does not give priority over other passengers.

Refunds not made.

Lost tickets not replaced.

The ticket remains the property of WMPTE and may be withdrawn by any of the named operators if it is misused.

This ticket to be produced on every journey. If not so produced, ordinary fares must be paid which are not refundable.

This ticket will be rendered invalid if altered, mutilated or defaced.

NOT TRANSFERABLE

NAME ....

ADDRESS ....

reverse

scholars

PRICE CODE **SC** — 130 000061

NOT VALID AFTER — 08 APR 62

CONDITIONS OF ISSUE, SEE OVERLEAF

2nd CLASS

NOT AVAILABLE FOR USE ON SATURDAYS AND SUNDAYS

◄◄ 16-18 Age Group Only

SC (H)

CONDITIONS OF ISSUE

Issued subject to the Regulations and Conditions in the Publications and Notices of the British Railways Board and the Published Terms and Conditions relating to the Executive and Midland Red's services and facilities which are available for inspection at the respective companies' head offices.

Valid on:
1. WMPTE and Midland Red service buses in the West Midlands County for journeys to or from school and in connection with the school curriculum.
2. Rail services between the points specified over (2nd class).

Valid Mondays to Fridays during school term only. Not valid after 2215 hours.

Does not give priority over other passengers.

Refunds not made.

Lost tickets not replaced.

The ticket remains the property of WMPTE and may be withdrawn by any of the named operators if it is misused.

This ticket to be produced on every journey. If not so produced, ordinary fares must be paid which are not refundable.

This ticket will be rendered invalid if altered, mutilated or defaced.

NOT TRANSFERABLE

NAME ....

Valid on Rail within the West Midlands County only

reverse

scholars

PRICE CODE **SD** — 701 001968

NOT VALID AFTER — 26 JUL 85

CONDITIONS OF ISSUE, SEE OVERLEAF

2nd CLASS

NOT AVAILABLE FOR USE ON SATURDAYS AND SUNDAYS

001 009581 ◄◄ Enter Identity Card Number (16-18 Age Group Only)

SD (H)

CONDITIONS OF ISSUE

Issued subject to the Regulations and Conditions in the Publications and Notices of the British Railways Board and the Published Terms and Conditions relating to the Executive and Midland Red's services and facilities which are available for inspection at the respective companies' head offices.

Valid on:
1. WMPTE and Midland Red service buses in the West Midlands County for journeys to or from school and in connection with the school curriculum, not later than 22.15 hrs.
2. Rail services within the West Midlands County Only (2nd Class).

Valid Mondays to Fridays during school term only. Not valid during holiday periods.

Does not give priority over other passengers.

Refunds not made.

Lost tickets not replaced.

The ticket remains the property of WMPTE and may be withdrawn by any of the named operators if it is misused.

This ticket to be produced on every journey. If not so produced, ordinary fares must be paid which are not refundable.

This ticket will be rendered invalid if altered, mutilated or defaced.

NOT TRANSFERABLE

NAME ....

ADDRESS ....

reverse

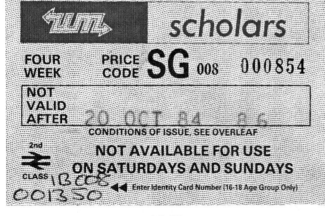

scholars

FOUR WEEK — PRICE CODE **SG** 008 — 000854

NOT VALID AFTER — 20 OCT 84

CONDITIONS OF ISSUE, SEE OVERLEAF

2nd CLASS

NOT AVAILABLE FOR USE ON SATURDAYS AND SUNDAYS

◄◄ Enter Identity Card Number (16-18 Age Group Only)

SG (E)

CONDITIONS OF ISSUE

Issued subject to the Regulations and Conditions in the Publications and Notices of the British Railways Board and the Published Terms and Conditions relating to the Executive and Midland Red's services and facilities which are available for inspection at the respective companies' head offices.

Valid on:
1. WMPTE and Midland Red service buses in the West Midlands County for journeys to or from school and in connection with the school curriculum, not later than 22.15 hrs.
2. Rail services within the West Midlands County Only (2nd Class).

Valid Mondays to Fridays during school term only. Not valid during holiday periods.

Does not give priority over other passengers.

Refunds not made.

Lost tickets not replaced.

The ticket remains the property of WMPTE and may be withdrawn by any of the named operators if it is misused.

This ticket to be produced on every journey. If not so produced, ordinary fares must be paid which are not refundable.

This ticket will be rendered invalid if altered, mutilated or defaced.

NOT TRANSFERABLE

NAME ....

ADDRESS ....

reverse

SG (E)

reverse

SL (H)

reverse

SL (E)

reverse

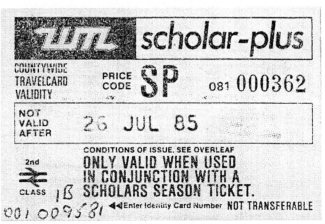

SP (E)

reverse

Staffs/Warwicks Scholar Ticket

ACADEMIC YEAR — PRICE CODE **SS** 711 — 000253

NOT VALID AFTER 27 JUL 84

NOT VALID SATURDAYS AND SUNDAYS. CONDITIONS OVERLEAF

Name ....

Address ....

School ....

SS (H)

reverse

Staffs/Warwicks Scholar Ticket

HALF-TERM — PRICE CODE **ST** 711 — 000333

NOT VALID AFTER 21 OCT 83

NOT VALID SATURDAYS AND SUNDAYS. CONDITIONS OVERLEAF

Name ....

Address ....

School ....

ST (H)

same reverse as SS

WMPTE Scholars Ticket publicity

WUMPTY'S LATEST FARE DEAL!

Scholars Ticket

for all school children and full-time students up to 18 years of age in West Midlands County.

Appendix A   WMPTE Ticket and Travelcard Prices
April 1983 - October 1986

Type			Price Code	Tickets introduced after 1 Apr 1983: Introduction date	Price	1Apr 1983 *	2Oct 1983	31Mar 1985	6Apr 1986
Travelcard	4 week	Child	F			£7.50	£7.50	£7.80	£9.00
Travelcard	4 week	Adult	G			£16.00	£16.00	£17.00	£19.50
Travelcard	1 week	Adult	L			£5.00	£5.00	£5.25	£6.00
Travelcard	1 week	Child	M			£2.50	£2.50	£2.60	£3.00
Travelcard	10 week	Student	U			£21 ?	-	-	-
Travelcard	10 week	Adult	U			-	£36.00	£40.00	£47.00
Travelcard	13 week	Adult	W			£46.50	£46.50	£52.50	£60.00
Travelcard	Annual	Adult	T	2 Jan 85	£180.00	-	-	£180.00	£200.00
Travelcard	School Term	Child	B	Sep 83	£21.00	-	£21.00	£22.00	£25.00
Travelcard	School Year	Child	A?	Sep 83	£65.00	-	£65.00	£70.00	£80.50
Travelcard Off Peak		Adult	OA			£5.00	£3.50	£3.50	£3.50
Travelcard Off Peak		Child	OB			£2.50	£1.75	£1.75	£1.75
Travelcard Off Peak Coventry		Adult	OC	27 Oct 85	£2.60	-	-	-	£2.60
Travelcard Off Peak Wolverhampton		Adult	ON	Apr 86	£2.60	-	-	-	-
Travelcard Off Peak Walsall		Adult	OL	Apr 86	£2.60	-	-	-	-
Travelcard Coventry	4 week	Adult	BE	Repriced 27 Oct 85	£12.50	£11.00	£11.00	£12.00	£14.00
Travelcard Coventry	1 week	Adult	BK	Repriced 27 Oct 85	£3.60	£3.25	£3.25	£3.50	£4.00
Travelcard Wolverhampton	4 week	Adult	CE			£11.00	£11.00	£12.00	£14.00
Travelcard Wolverhampton	1 week	Adult	CK			£3.25	£3.25	£3.50	£4.00
Travelcard Walsall	4 week	Adult	DE			£11.00	£11.00	£12.00	£14.00
Travelcard Walsall	1 week	Adult	DK			£3.25	£3.25	£3.50	£4.00
Daytripper		Family	Q			£3.00	£2.75	£2.75	£2.75
Daytripper		Adult	QA			£2.00	£1.50	£1.50	£1.50
Daytripper		Child	QC			£1.00	£0.75	£0.75	£0.75
Supertripper		Family	QG	May 86	£4.50	-	-	-	-
Supertripper		Adult	QH	May 86	£2.25	-	-	-	-
Supertripper		Child	QJ	May 86	£1.25	-	-	-	-
Supertripper		Senior Citizen	QK	May 86	£1.25	-	-	-	-
Coventry & Warwicks Day Out		Family	QW	Jul 83	£5.00	-	£5.00	£5.00	-
Coventry & Warwicks Day Out		Adult	QX	Jul 83	£3.00	-	£3.00	£3.00	-
Coventry & Warwicks Day Out		Child	QY	Jul 83	£1.90	-	£1.90	£1.90	-
Airlink		Adult	QZ	? 83	£1.50	-	-	£1.50	-
Southern Rider		Family	QF	25 May 85	£6.00	-	-	-	-
Southern Rider		Adult	QD	25 May 85	£3.00	-	-	-	-
Southern Rider		Junior	QE	25 May 85	£1.90	-	-	-	-
Easy Rider		Adult	R	From 5 Nov 83	£7.00	£6.50	£6.50	£7.00	£7.00
				From 20 Apr 86	£8.80				
Easy Rider Registration Fee			-			£0.25	£0.25	?	?
Travelcard Registration Fee			-			£0.75	£0.85	£0.85	£0.85

* 7 Mar 1982 fare increase, except for tickets introduced between this date and 1 Apr 1983.

Appendix B   Ticket Machines used by WMPTE

During the period April 1983 to October 1986 WMPTE used three types of ticket machine - or perhaps we should use a more modern expression and call them "fare collection systems" or something like that!

One of these was **Autofare I**, which had been in use since 1970 and which was fully described in *Part 1* of *"Tickets of the West Midlands PTE, 1969-1983."* From 1983 onwards, this system was gradually phased out in favour of Autofare 3, but survived in ever-declining numbers until October 1986 - much longer than expected.

Autofare 3

A brief description of this electronic ticket issuing and revenue control system was provided in *Part 1*, but by courtesy of the manufacturers, Control Systems Ltd., a fuller account can now be given here. WMPTE introduced Autofare 3 in May 1982 at West Bromwich Garage, fitted to a batch of brand new MCW Metrobus Mk II double deckers. All subsequent buses of this type were so equipped, and from 1983 onwards most other buses were converted to this system.

Like Autofare 1, it consists of basically three units:

1) A Farebox, into which the passenger was politely expected to drop the exact fare. Having (in theory) checked it, the driver pressed a button which released the money into a locked vault below, and simultaneously issued a ticket from another unit positioned nearby. WMPTE retained the same fareboxes as they used with Autofare 1.

2) A Keyboard Module operated by the driver. This is the brainbox of the system and contains a microprocessor.

   Autofare 3 can be used in four different operating "modes":

   a) Rapid Issue Mode. This is the normal method of operation, whereby the driver can issue tickets for the most common fares, by pressing the appropriate "dedicated" key on a row of ten. Ten further fares can be selected by using an additional key.

   b) Fixed Mode. For flat fare services, the keyboard can be made to issue tickets of the same value by pressing a single key. By pressing the "Clear" key, the driver can switch back to Rapid Issue.

   c) Tickets for additional fares (i.e. those not covered by the 10 "dedicated" keys) can be issued by entering the class and amount.

   d) WMPTE were never able to make use of this fourth facility, but machines could be programmed with route / fare table information. The driver would advance the boarding stage number as the journey progressed, then, by entering the required Class and destination stage number, the machine would issue a ticket of the correct fare. The ticket could display (by stage name) the furthest point of travel to which it was valid. See Fig 101 on Page 65.

   The Keyboard can also be used to issue Waybill information, and (by using a VHF radio link) can transfer the information direct to a central computer at the operator's offices or garage.

3) The third basic component of Autofare 3 is the Ticket Issuing Module - i.e. the large red box from which the ticket appears. When the driver presses the key, it takes less than one second for the ticket to be printed and ejected.

The early Autofare 3 machines, as used by WMPTE, were later modified by fitting a "cup" (similar to those on the Autofare 1 machines) over the mouthpiece. Hitherto, the ticket had simply protruded from a slot. All subsequent machines followed the modified pattern.

Autofare 3 tickets are produced in the form of large rolls, rather than the folded packs used for Autofare 1. According to the maker's specifications, tickets have a minimum length of 57 mm and a maximum length of 100 mm, with a standard width of 30 mm. WMPTE's tickets were always 85 mm in length.

The third type of ticket machine was:

Almex Model P

In October 1985 WMPTE placed in service 10 Ford Transit minibuses, based at the Central Coachways garage in Walsall. They were used on services in the Kingstanding (Birmingham) and West Bromwich areas, and were fitted with Almex ticket machines. WMPTE had inherited a number of Almex "A" machines from Birmingham, West Bromwich and Wolverhampton Corporations, but these had all disappeared by 1976.

The 1985 machines are understood to have been Model P. They had a short life with WMPTE, being used up until Deregulation and then replaced by Wayfarer II machines.

WMPTE did not use Wayfarer II machines, so no description is attempted here. However their successor, West Midlands Travel Ltd., introduced them on Deregulation Day itself, fitted to new minibuses. As far as I know, West Midlands Travel did not use either Autofare 1 or Almex, although both types remained in use with WMPTE right up until Deregulation or just before it.

Appendix C   Sales Point Codes

Sales Point Codes (or Outlet Codes) were introduced in 1979, and subsequently appeared on all Travelcards, Family Day Tickets, Coventry & Warwickshire Day Outs, Daytrippers, Supertrippers, Southern Riders, Easy Riders and Scholars Tickets. They are the small 3-figure codes printed immediately to the left of the serial number, and they indicated the WMPTE office, BR Station or other agency from which the ticket was purchased.

The following list was kindly provided by WMPTE, and shows the position as at 17th July 1986. I have re-arranged the details in a slightly different layout (with Agents' addresses abbreviated), and have reinstated a small number of outlets which had been manually deleted from the PTE's list. Readers may have tickets showing codes which are not listed, as inevitably some codes became obsolete over the years. Codes which are known to have been used have been added to the list, but in some cases I am unable to identify the meaning.

One anomaly is code 212, which is listed as a Birmingham newsagent, but which can be found on many Coventry Travelcards. This code seems to have changed its meaning at some stage, and I suggest - without any actual proof - that 212 (when related to Coventry issues) should be treated as 412. (i.e. Devlins in Broadgate.)

To avoid any possible confusion, it should be remembered that there were two quite separate "sales outlets" at Birmingham (New Street) station - the BR ticket window, and the PTE's own renewal office.

The availability of "Add-on" Travelcards and Supertrippers helps to explain why so many railway stations outside the WM County were allocated Sales Point Codes.

Using the following list, readers will (in most cases) be able to identify the particular office or agency where their Travelcards etc. were sold, and this should add a bit of interest.

001-099. WMPTE Travel Centres, Enquiry Offices, etc.

001, 021, 031 } 041, 051, 061 } 071, 081, 091 }	Paradise Place, Birmingham - by Central Library
002, 022, 032 } 042, 052, 062 } 072 }	Birmingham (New Street) Station - WMPTE office.
003, 033, 043 } 053, 063. }	Walsall
004, 024, 034 } 044, 054 }	Coventry
005, 025, 035	Solihull
006	Sutton Coldfield
007, 047, 057	Wolverhampton
008, 048, 058	West Bromwich
009, 017, 049	Dudley
011, 016	Oldbury
012, 018, 019	Sales Administration
014	Wolverhampton?

101-199 British Rail Stations

101	Longbridge
102	Northfield
103	Kings Norton
104	Bournville
105	Selly Oak
106	University
107	Berkswell
108	Tile Hill
109	Canley
110	Coventry
111	Wolverhampton
112	Coseley
113	Tipton
114	Dudley Port
115	Sandwell & Dudley (known as Oldbury until 1984)
116	Smethwick Rolfe Street
117	Smethwick West
118	Langley Green
119	Rowley Regis
120	Old Hill
121	Cradley Heath
122	Lye
123	Stourbridge Junction
124	Stourbridge Town
125	Acocks Green
126	Olton
127	Solihull
128	Dorridge
129	Spring Road
130	Hall Green
131	Yardley Wood
132	Shirley
133	Wythall
134	Birmingham New Street
135	Birmingham Moor Street
136	Small Heath
137	Tyseley
138	Adderley Park
139	Stechford
140	Lea Hall
141	Marston Green
142	Birmingham International
143	Hampton in Arden
144	Duddeston
145	Aston
146	Witton
147	Perry Barr
148	Hamstead
149	Bescot
150	Walsall
151	Gravelly Hill
152	Erdington
153	Chester Road
154	Wylde Green
155	Sutton Coldfield
156	Four Oaks
157	Butlers Lane
158	Blake Street
159	Five Ways
160	Birmingham International
161	(Not used?)
162	Redditch
163	Lapworth
164	Hatton
165	Warwick
166	Leamington
167	Henley in Arden
168	Wilmcote (Deleted)
169	Stratford upon Avon
170	Hagley
171	Kidderminster
172	Shenstone
173	Lichfield
174	(Not used?)
175	Stafford
176	Birmingham New Street
177	Birmingham New Street
178	Birmingham New Street
179	Water Orton
180	Coventry
181	Bilbrook
182	Codsall
183	Albrighton
184	Cosford
185	Shifnal
186	Oakengates
187	Wellington
188	Shrewsbury

189	Bromsgrove	
190	Droitwich	
191	Worcester Shrub Hill	
192	Worcester Foregate Street	
193	Telford Central	
194	Evesham	
195	Malvern Link	
196	Great Malvern	
197	Rugby	
198	Long Buckby	
199	Northampton	

It is understood that Codes 176-178 were used only on Daytrippers and possibly Supertrippers, but not Travelcards.

200 Series. Agents in the former South Division (i.e. Birmingham area)

200	Sandhu News	Chelmsley Wood
201	G. B. Singh	Chelmsley Wood
202	Shakir	Oakhurst Rd., Birmingham 27
203	NSS	Warwick Rd., Birmingham 27
204	?	
205	Yew Tree P.O.	Yardley
206	Village Stores	Bartley Green
207	JM Leeson	Burlington Passage, Bimingham 2
208	City Centre Kiosk	Union St., Birmingham 2
209	News Kiosks	Colmore Circus Precinct, B'ham 4
210	Midland Red	Birmingham Bus Station
211	?	
212	Preedy's	Tile Cross Rd., Birmingham 33
213	NSS	Chester Road, Birmingham 36
214	C. J. Jones News	Chester Road, Birmingham 36
215	Jays News	Falkland Way, Birmingham 36
216	NSS	Cotteridge
217	Stars News	Druids Heath
218	Martins	Five Ways, Birmingham 12
219	Stars News	Erdington
220	S. Mir	Hall Green
221	B. R. Patel News	Erdington
222	J & D Moore	Castle Bromwich
223	Great Barr News	Great Barr
224	Randhawa News	Bordesley Green
225	Cannon Hill News	Balsall Heath
226	Dillons	Castle Vale
227	Preedy's	Kitts Green
228	West's Newsagents	West Heath
229	Sall	Handsworth
230	Heer	Handsworth
231	Satchwell	Great Barr
232	Princes News	Harborne
233	J.J. Chauhan News	Hay Mills
234	Dillons	Kings Heath
235	Fortunoff	Kings Heath
236	NSS	Kings Norton
237	Lavells	Perry Barr
238	Clare Travel	Kingstanding
239	Kirtons	Kingstanding
240	D. Maddocks	Knowle
241	?	
242	Dillons	Castle Bromwich
243	F. & H. Axford	Maypole
244	James Travel	Hall Green
245	Nayyar	Moseley
246	Brighton Rd. P.O.	Moseley
247	Bosworth Travel	Moseley
248	?	
249	John Frost	Sutton Coldfield
250	Dillons	Northfield
251	N. T. News	Selly Park
252	Bange	Perry Barr
253	Bowen	Bearwood Rd., Warley (Deleted)
254	O'Brien	Quinton
255	Villa Cross News	Lozells
256	Polly's	Rubery
257	Mistry News	Saltley
258	Virdi News	Selly Oak
259	Samra News	Stechford
260	Sammons News	Bordesley Green
261	NSS	Sheldon
262	Stars News	Shirley

263	Harrison's	Small Heath
264	B & P News	Small Heath
265	Axfords	Small Heath
266	Lady Pool News	Sparkbrook
267	Mistry	South Yardley
268	Nayyar	Acocks Green
269	Shetland News	Sparkbrook
270	Pelham News	Alum Rock Rd., Birmingham 8
271	The Bon Bon	Erdington
272	Soho News	Handsworth
273	A & R. D. Leake	Stirchley
274	Nationwide News	Sutton Coldfield
275	Gardner	Sutton Coldfield
276	James Travel	Sparkhill
277	?	
278	F. Kilby	Ward End
279	P. Peel	Ward End
280	Sidhu	Washwood Heath
281	NSS	Weoley Castle
282	K. P. News	Edgbaston
283	Pal Bros.	Witton
284	Stars News	Wylde Green
285	Job & Sons	Garretts Green Lane, B"ham 26
286	Job & Sons	Coventry Road, Birmingham 26
287	F. & H. Axford	Yardley
288	Stars News	Yardley
289	F. & H.Axford	Yardley Wood
290	Galleon Wine	Shard End
291	?	
292	?	
293	J. Leeson	Hurst St. (Subway Kiosk), B'ham 5
294	Fortunoff	Northfield
295	Johal News	Great Barr
296	Seddons	Erdington

300 Series. Agents in the former North Division (Black Country & neighbouring areas)

300	Greens Tours & Travel	Stourbridge
301	Bearwood News	Bearwood
302	Anchor News	Aldridge
303	Mistry Bros.	Beeches Rd., Walsall
304	Dillons	Bloxwich
305	Greens Tours & Travel	Brierley Hill
306	Stars News	Gornal Wood
307	A. F. Parsons	Darlaston
308	M. Cliff	Stone St., Dudley
309	J & S News	Blackheath
310	Dilsur News	Halesowen
311	The Wool Shop	Wednesfield
312	Stars News	Pelsall
313	Likeman Agency	Hednesford
314	Preedy's	Cannock
315	Meachems Stores & P.O.	Burntwood
316	S. K. Shuckla	High St., Smethwick
317	J. R. Holyhead	Willenhall
318	Janagal News	Wednesbury
319	J. S. Stores	Bilston
320	S. Clohessy	Great Barr
321	Stars News	Ashmore Park
322	B. J. Adams	Carters Green, West Bromwich
323	Preedy's	Bilston (Deleted)
324	Thomas Cook	Halesowen
325	C. P. News (Previously A. J. Perry)	
		Wulfruna St., Wolverhampton
326	?	
327	Merry Hill P. O.	Wolverhampton
328	Summerhill Travel	Stafford Rd., Wolverhampton
329	Preedy's (Previously at Midland Educational Co.)	
		Wulfrun Way, Wolverhampton
330	Haden News	Sedgley
331	Summerhill Travel	Kingswinford
332	Joy News	Waterloo Rd., Smethwick
333	KGS News	Halesowen
334	Burntwood News	Burntwood

400 Series. Agents in the former East Division (Coventry)

400	G. Eld	Moseley Avenue
401	NSS	Jubilee Crescent
402	Funnell	Station St., East

403	Pennywise	Quinton Park
404	NSS	Belgrave Rd.
405	Devlins	Cross Cheaping
406	C. Dunford	Hall Green Rd.
407	?	
408	Devlins	Shelton Square
409	E. Jones & Son	Princethorpe Way
410	NSS	Jardine Crescent
411	Toll Bar Newsagents	St. James Lane
412	Devlins	Broadgate
413	J. Hulm	Aldermoor Lane

500/600/900 series. Miscellaneous Agencies

500	University of Birmingham	
501	University of Aston (Deleted)	
502	Birmingham Polytechnic	
503	County Hall, Birmingham	
504	D. J. Loone,	Beake Ave., Coventry
505	University of Warwick	Coventry
510	Hanlon	Birmingham Airport (Deleted)

600	Midland Red (?) (Deleted)	
602	Midland Red North	Lichfield Bus Station

900	S. J. Hardwick-Dawson	Chasetown
903	NEC Arena Theatre	National Exhibition Centre
905	Information Desk, Birmingham International Airport	

700 Series. Education Authorities or Schools

701	Birmingham
702	Coventry
703	Sandwell
704	Dudley
705	Solihull
706	Walsall
707	Wolverhampton
708	Wolverhampton
709	County of Hereford & Worcester
710	Staffordshire
711	Warwickshire (Nuneaton)
712	Warwickshire (Warwick)

726	King Edward's School, Aston
727	Bishop Vesey's School, Sutton Coldfield
729	Handsworth Grammar School
732	King Edward's School, Kings Heath

This series was mainly for Scholars Tickets, but some of the schools issued Young Persons Travelcards as well.

WMPTE Travelcard publicity

For as long as anyone can remember, bus and tram tickets have tended to carry a wide variety of advertisements on the back, just as the vehicles themselves would often display adverts on the outside and inside, front and rear. Ticket adverts must have covered virtually every item or service, ranging from coffee to corsets, beer to bicycles, tombstones to toothpaste, etc etc! Nowadays, just as in the "old days" these adverts provide a valuable source of revenue for operators and (in a world where so much has changed) they perhaps form a line of continuity between past and present.

Yet strangely enough, the study and research of advertisements is still a very neglected aspect of the ticket collecting hobby. A number of enthusiastic collectors have devoted a lot of time to the subject - and have probably never received due acknowledgement for their efforts. Bell Punch-printed tickets, back in those sadly lamented "good old days," usually displayed "block numbers" which (to those with access to the necessary information) would help to date both the advert and the ticket.

Then there was the fascinating range of wartime slogans ("Be like Dad, keep Mum" etc.) followed in more peaceful times by such classics as "Typhoo Tea for Indigestion" and "Littlewoods Pools."

Who can say whether all these dim and distant adverts have been faithfully recorded and preserved for posterity? What of the more recent offerings, on Ultimates, T.I.Ms, Setrights, etc?

In my own small way, I tried to record all the adverts to be found on WMPTE Autofare 3 tickets - but I'm sure that I missed at least a few of them. On the next few pages are illustrated all the examples recorded by the writer, mostly dating between April 1984 and October 1986. Some of the later adverts appeared both on WMPTE-titled tickets and subsequently on West Midlands Travel issues, but (sadly) a number of rather attractive adverts had to be omitted from our survey because I could only find them on WMT-titled issues! I could, of course, have cheated here - and I'm sure no-one would have known any different!

It all started in May 1982, with the first of the PTE's Autofare 3 tickets, initially used at West Bromwich Garage but quickly spread all over the system. These carried the wording "West Mids PTE proudly present the new Autofare 3 ticketing system," shown alongside the famous Control Systems Ltd. address, The Island, Uxbridge.

Then, in April 1984 came the first of several adverts for the "Night Out" club in Birmingham. These, incidentally, were probably unique by being in two colours, cerise and blue.

Many adverts tended to be blue (i.e. blue lettering!), but a lot reappeared in green, red, cerise or black.

In May 1984 appeared the first of several series (in different colours) featuring "adverts for adverts." These consisted of a string of little slogans, such as "Why not advertise in this space" or "Your advertisement could be here," with a telephone number underneath. These will be of little interest to readers, so (for reasons of space) I have only illustrated one or two specimen examples.

A simple, but rather attractive early advert was "Simply bags of shopping at City of Birmingham Markets," which appeared in red in August 1984, but changed to blue in December.

"Keep your buses and trains" (January 1985) was, of course, a political slogan defending WMPTE and the WM County Council against the Government's proposal to abolish them. Perhaps it didn't occur to them that the slogan could be read in two ways!

I don't intend to describe each advert individually - the illustrations will do that perfectly well, though they will not, of course, reflect the changes of colour which occurred, mainly in 1986.

Initially it was quite easy to keep a record of these adverts, together with an accurate pinpointing of the month of introduction. They came along at a fairly leisurely rate, with just one advert throughout each ticket roll. Until December 1985, tickets are illustrated with the month of introduction underneath.

But in that month the situation suddenly snowballed, with new adverts coming through thick and fast, and with several designs on each ticket roll. These were less easy to record, and I freely admit that I probably missed a few. Tickets without a date of introduction can be assumed to be between December 1985 and October 1986. I have tried to marshal them in vaguely chronological order, but this is not really feasible.

It would be nice to be able to claim that an advert for (let's say) a Wolverhampton shop was used only or mainly on tickets issued in Wolverhampton, but this was not the case, and (certainly after December 1985) would not have been practicable. The general rule seems to have been that adverts were used willy-nilly all over the WMPTE system. I know of only one apparent exception to this, and I may well be wrong, but it seems that the red "Pass on your Postcode" advert of May 1985 was only used in Coventry. There was a Postcode advert-bus running in that city around that period.

So here they are, lined up before your eyes - pawnbrokers to pregnancy tests, battered cats and clever little pigs, leaking roofs and burglar alarms. We even have a couple of naked lovers - but in the best possible taste, of course!

CONTROL SYSTEMS LIMITED	WEST MIDS P.T.E.
THE ISLAND UXBRIDGE MIDDLESEX UB8 2UT TEL: UXBRIDGE 51255	PROUDLY PRESENT THE NEW AUTOFARE 3 TICKETING SYSTEM

May 1982

"NIGHT·OUT"   "NIGHT·O

SEE "THE DRIFTERS"   SEE "THE DRIFTER
WK. JUNE 5TH.   WK. JUNE 5TH
WITH   WITH
JOHNNY MOORE+BEN E. KING   JOHNNY MOORE+BEN
£2P.P WITH THIS TICKET   £2P.P. WITH THIS T
TELEPHONE OR CALL   TELEPHONE OR C
021-622 2233   021-622 2233

April 1984

LET THIS ADVERTISEMENT SELL YOUR COMPANY Tel 021 454 1156	WHY NOT ADVERTISE IN THIS SPACE Tel 021 454 1156

May 1984 - Six slogans (blue) ....

THE TICKET THE ...ISING TICKET ...21 454 1156	YOUR ADVERTISEMENT COULD BE HERE Tel 021 454 1156	LE... ADVER... SELL YO... Tel 0...

.... reappeared in red May 1985

HT OUT'   'NIGHT OUT'

ERNARD MANNING"   SEE "BERNARD MANNING"

12TH. 13TH. 14TH.   JULY 12TH. 13TH. 14TH.

H THIS TICKET   £2P P WITH THIS TICKET
ONE OR CALL   TELEPHONE OR CALL
-622 2233   021-622 2233

June 1984

'NIGHT OUT'   'NIGHT O

T GOSSIP & FRANKIE HOWERD   HOT GOSSIP & FRANKIE H

ES. 7TH. AUGUST TO FRI. 10TH.   TUES. 7TH. AUGUST TO FR

T £2P P WITH THIS TICKET   £2P P
TELEPHONE OR CALL   TE
021-622 2233

July 1984

SHOPPING   SIMPLY BAGS OF SHOPPING   SIMPLY
AT
F   CITY OF
MARKETS   BIRMINGHAM MARKETS   BIRMI
OVER
LS!   1100 STALLS!

August 1984 (red), December 1984 (blue)

OU SEEN THE   HAVE YOU SEEN THE
VON   AVON
EMENT ON T.V.?   ADVERTISEMENT ON T.V.
ME TO START EARNING   NOW IS THE TIME TO START
EY FOR CHRISTMAS.   EXTRA MONEY FOR CHRIST
WISH TO SELL, OR BUY,   WHETHER YOU WISH TO SELL,
8603 OR 021-554-1499   'PHONE 021-554-8603 OR 021-5

October 1984

'NIGHT OUT'   'NIGHT O

THE THREE DEGREES   THE THREE D
WED. 2ND. & THURS. 3RD. JAN.   WED. 2ND. & THUR
ALSO   ALSO
MON. TO THURS. 7TH. TO 10TH. JAN.   MON. TO THURS. 7TH
£3 SHOW ONLY WITH THIS TICKET   £3 SHOW ONLY WIT
TELEPHONE OR CALL THE BOX OFFICE   TELEPHONE OR CALL
021-622 2233   021-622 2

November 1984

CT HARMONY   SKILL & SCISSORS IN PERFECT HARMONY
Hair City One
SEX SALON)   (THE FRIENDLIEST UNISEX SALON)
THIS TICKET   20% DISCOUNT WITH THIS TICKET
26   PHONE 236 5426
R CENTRE   JEWELLERY & SILVER CENTRE
CKLEY B18.   SPENCER STREET, HOCKLEY B18.

November 1984

S   AL'S GENTS HAIRDRESSERS   AL'S G
N   161. RESERVOIR ROAD, STOCKLAND GREEN   161. RES
T   ARE OFFERING YOU A 10% DISCOUNT   ARE OFF
WITH THIS TICKET!!   TEL. 021-384 7456   WITH TH

November 1984

RENNI'S
Fashions
EAR,   LADIES EXCLUSIVE DAY WEAR,   L
NGS   EVENING WEAR, WEDDINGS
RE   ALSO MADE TO MEASURE
REEN,   199, DUDLEY RD., WINSON GREEN,   19
BIRMINGHAM B18 7QY
TEL. 021 454 0856

December 1984

December 1984

PORKIES   BRING THIS TICKET IN FOR 10p OFF
EVERY £1.00.   PORK
THE BEST IN U.S. STYLE 100% BEEF
HAMBURGERS

KENTUCKY STYLE CHICKEN AND FRIES ... ... 89p   KENTUCKY STYLE CH

JUMBO HOT DOGS, 8" LONG, ALL PORK ... ... 59p   JUMBO HOT DOGS, 8"

TRADITIONAL BLACK COUNTRY HOT PORK BUNS, WITH HOT ROAST   TRADITIONAL BLACK
PORK, STUFFING, CRACKLING, GRAVY AND MUSTARD ... ... 59p   PORK, STUFFING, CRA

December 1984

YOUR BUSES   KEEP YOUR BUSES
D TRAINS-   AND TRAINS-
EST MIDLANDS   KEEP WEST MIDLANDS
NTY COUNCIL   COUNTY COUNCIL

January 1985

18 PLUS   18 P
for everyone 18-30   for everyo
18 PLUS JOIN US!   18 PLUS JOIN
18 PLUS, PO BOX 77, BIRMINGHAM   18 PLUS, PO BOX 77, BI

January 1985

February 1985

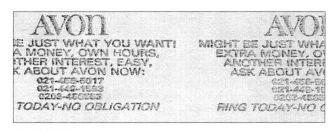

April 1985

May 1985 - red

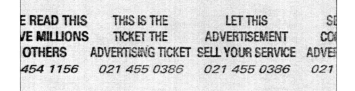

*June 1985 - second series - blue; June 1985 cerise,
September 1985 black*

June 1985

August 1985

September 1985 - black

4th series (3rd not illustrated)

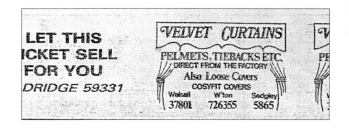

*Sticker placed on Autofare 3 ticket dispensing
units when the ticket roll was exhausted.*

The idea of this list is for collectors to "tick off" the items in their collections. Subject to accidental omissions, it includes all WMPTE-titled tickets mentioned for the first time in this publication, plus certain other tickets not actually issued by the PTE, but associated with them. One or two "fringe" items have been excluded. Not an easy list to compile, one problem being that the situation does not lend itself to chronological order.

Autofare 3

Set	Description	Machine number
A11	Guided Bus	
A12	Thin paper	
-	Thrufare Adult	
-	Thrufare Child	

Almex Model P

Machine number

Miscellaneous Tickets

Description		✓
Coventry Air Display 1976 - Adult		
Coventry Air Display 1976 - Child		
Coventry Area 2p Prepaid c1974		
Easy Rider £7 (red value figure)		
Easy Rider £7 (black value figure)		
Easy Rider £8.80		
Coventry and Warwicks Day Out	QW	
Coventry and Warwicks Day Out	QX	
Coventry and Warwicks Day Out	QY	
Walsall Garage Open Day 1983		
Airlink	QZ	
Rotary Travelcard 1984		
Leisure Rider 1984		
SPACE ticket 1984		
Southern Rider - Family		
Southern Rider - Adult		
Southern Rider - Junior		
London Liner coach ticket		
Supertripper - Family		
Supertripper - Adult		
Supertripper - Child		
Supertripper - Senior Citizen		
Blind/Disabled Pass (any type)		
Representative's Pass		
City Sightseeing Tour £2 yellow		
City Sightseeing Tour £1.50 blue		
City Sightseeing Tour £1 orange		

Daytripper

Price code	Type	Card/paper	Showing years	✓
QA	Adult	Card	1983-4-5	
QC	Child	Card	1983-4-5	
Q	Family	Paper	1983-4-5	
QA	Adult	Paper	1983-4-5	
QC	Child	Paper	1983-4-5	
Q	Family	Paper	1984-5-6	
QA	Adult	Paper	1984-5-6	
QC	Child	Paper	1984-5-6	
Q	Family	Paper	1985-6-7	
QA	Adult	Paper	1985-6-7	
QC	Child	Paper	1985-6-7	

Travelcards

Design	Price Code	Back block	SA ✓	SB ✓
Tc262	G	O		
Tc262	G	P		
Tc281	U	Q		
Tc292	W	U		
Tc292A	W	R		
Tc293	W	Q		
Tc296	F	Q		
Tc322A	BE	C4		
Tc325	BK	C1		
Tc342	CE	WN3		
Tc361A	DE	WL1		
Tc365A	DK	WL1		
Tc405	OA	OP2		
Tc406	OB	OP2		
Tc421	OC	OP3		
Tc422	OC	OP3		
Tc431	OL	OP4		
Tc441	ON	OP5		
Tc491	B	Q		
Tc501	F	Q		
Tc511	G	Q		
Tc521	L	Q		
Tc522	L	Q		
Tc531	M	Q		
Tc541	S	S		
Tc551	T	T		
Tc561	U	Q		
Tc561A	U	R		
Tc601	BE	C4		
Tc611	BK	C4		
Tc621	CE	WN2		
Tc631	CK	WN2		
Tc632	CK	WN2		
Tc641	DE	WL1		
Tc651	DK	WL1		
Tc652	DK	WL1		

SA = Serial number **a**longside Price Code
SB = Serial number **b**elow level of Price Code

Scholars Passes etc
Listed as per illustration figure numbers in Chapter 5

Figure Number	✓
50	
52	
54	
56	
58	
60	
62	
64	
65	
67	
69	
70	

Scholars Tickets

Price Code	Bemrose	Booth
SA		
SB		
SC		
SD		
SE		
SG		
SL		
SP		
SS		
ST		
SU		

Walsall District Prepaid
Scholars Weekly Season Tickets

Red printing	✓
2/6d	
3/2d	
23p	
30p	
38p	
45p	

Black printing	✓
13p	
16p	
19p	
32p	
45p	

Pensioners Passes
Listed as per illustration figure numbers in Chapter 4

Figure Number	✓
43	
44	
(card passes)	
45	
46	
(plastic passes)	

Date	Chapter	Event
1983		
Jun 1983	1	Conversion of fleet from Autofare 1 to Autofare 3 commenced.
Jul 1983	2	Introduction of "Coventry and Warwickshire Day Out" tickets.
24 Jul 1983	2	Special ticket for Walsall Garage Open Day.
8 Aug 1983	5	Introduction of Photocards.
2 Oct 1983	1	Off-Peak fares system introduced.
5 Nov 1983	2	Easy Rider price increased.
28 Dec 1983	4	Afternoon and evening restrictions on Pensioners Passes abolished.
1984		
Apr 1984	1	First advertisements appear on Autofare 3 tickets.
1 Jun 1984	2	Rotary Travelcard introduced.
Jul 1984	3	Introduction of Costclipper discount scheme.
30 Jul 1984	2	Introduction of Leisure Rider tickets.
9 Oct 1984	1	Inauguration of Guided Bus scheme using special Autofare 3 tickets.
1985		
7 Jan 1985	1	Return tickets available on Walsall-Lichfield service (901).
Mar 1985	1	Appearance of class indication on Autofare 3 tickets.
7 Apr 1985	1	First day of Civil Wars Heritage Tours (special tickets).
25 May 1985	2	Introduction of Southern Rider tickets, replacing Coventry and Warwickshire Day Out tickets.
28 Jul 1985	1	"Thrufare" 50p ticket introduced.
14 Oct 1985	1	Shuttlebus minibus service introduced using Almex Model P machines.
27 Oct 1985	3	Coventry Off-Peak Travelcard introduced.
c24 Nov 1985	3	Travelcards reinstated in part of Staffordshire and also in the County of Hereford and Worcester.
1986		
17 Mar 1986	2	London Liner coach service inaugurated.
Apr 1986	3	Off-Peak Area Travelcards for Wolverhampton and Walsall.
May 1986	2	Introduction of Supertripper.
26 Jun 1986	3	Reinstatement of Travelcard on most of remaining services in Staffordshire - principally routes running from Walsall. Also Walsall Travelcards and Walsall Off-Peak Travelcards extended to incorporate Cannock area.
Jul 1986	2	Easy Rider tickets withdrawn by WMPTE.
25 Oct 1986	1	Last day of bus operation by WMPTE.

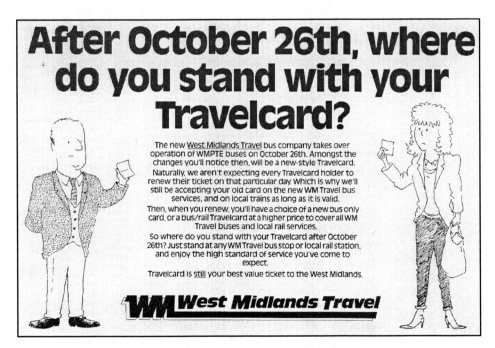

Leaflet explaining Travelcard validity post-Deregulation - 26 October 1986

Appendix G   Additions and Corrections to Parts 1-3

In 1984, The Transport Ticket Society published "*Tickets of the West Midlands PTE, 1969-1983*" in three separate parts, namely:

> *Part 1: Machine-issued Tickets.*
> *Part 2: Miscellaneous Tickets.*
> *Part 3: Travelcards.*

Inevitably, perhaps, a few printing errors escaped correction. Most of these are trivial and obvious for what they are, but one or two had the effect of altering or obscuring the meaning of the sentence. Also, a small number of readers kindly contacted the writer to point out mistakes or to provide additional information, and I have myself discovered new sources of information which correct, amplify (or merely cast doubt upon!) what has gone before.

Additional information (as opposed to corrections or queries) is followed by "(A)." So here goes:

Part 1 Machine-issued Tickets.

Page 7   I have not been able to compile a full list, by any means, of those ex-BMMO Setright machines which were repurchased by Midland Red, but they include the following numbers: 0136, 0149, 0477, 0512, 0544, 0569, 0605/7/9, 0618, 0622/5, 0644/7/9, 0650/3/6, 0703, 0733, 0823/9, 0855/7/8, 1000, 1018, 1025/8, 1060/8, 1109, 1121/4, 1249, 1262, 1388 and 1394.   (A)

Page 8   It seems that BCT T.I.M.s were used mainly on Routes 43 (Nechells), 46 (Queslett), 69 (Lozells), 98 (Kingstanding, Limited Stop) and 99 (Rubery, Limited Stop).   (A)

Page 9   (Penultimate paragraph). Birmingham Almex machines 0021-0024 *were* used. It seems likely that they were also transferred to Wolverhampton District, together with 0001-0020. Were 0025-0027 used by BCT?

Appendix A   (1) On line 2 of paragraph 2, "a roll ticket" should, of course, read "a ticket roll"!

Appendix A   (6) Transport Services serial numbers progressed in *Barca*rolle method. i.e. Aa, Ba, Ca, etc.   (A)

Appendix B   (1) Paragraph 2, line 5. Insert the word "perhaps" in the space between "with" and "advertisements."

Appendix B   (2) Evidence suggests that Type WM1 tickets could be found in use until July 1975 at least.

Appendix D   (2) Paragraph 4, line 4, should read: "There are possibly four different styles ..."

Part 2 Miscellaneous Tickets

Page 6   Ticket prices for the 1978 Motor Show were as follows:

	Adult	Child
From anywhere in the WM County (Bus / Rail / Admission)	£2.00	£1.45
From Birmingham New St. (Rail / Admission)	£1.55	£1.25
From Coventry (Rail / Admission)	£1.60	£1.25
(Reduced prices from stations between Adderley Park and Berkswell) Admission tickets only (purchased from railway stations)	£1.00	-

(A)

The 1978 Exhibitors ticket should be added to the Checklist.

Page 9   Mention is made of the BCT guide book for the Outer Circle Route, issued in the 1920's. In 1985, the Birmingham Urban Studies Committee published a new guide book for this route, as part of their series of "Brum Trails," and for the cover they used a facsimile of the 1927 guide, depicting two open-staircase AECs. "See Birmingham's charming suburbs by bus," says the original wording. "25 miles for fifteen pence." Not 15p, but 15 real pence - in other words, 1/3d! The 1985 guide cost 75p from the Tourist Information Centre.   (A)

Page 13   The wording on Papal tickets E and F was actually "RAIL AND SHUTTLE BUS ONLY."

Two additional (and very rare) types should be added to the Checklist, as types G and H. These are identical to E and F but carry a sticker over the bottom panel, saying "VALID ADDITIONALLY BY BUS BETWEEN SHELDON WHEATSHEAF AND INTERNATIONAL STATION."

Apparently produced for use by staff and pupils of St. Thomas More's R. C. School, Horse Shoes Lane, Sheldon, Birmingham. (A)

Page 13   The Price Code Q Daytripper was first seen by the writer in February 1984, and was light green (not silver, as anticipated) with dark green printing, and on paper rather than card. Price Code Q tickets do not exist on card.

Additional types of Miscellaneous Card and Paper tickets:-

1) By courtesy of Bob Davis (who also provided specimens of all WMPTE Papal tickets), I can illustrate two tickets produced by WMPTE (East Division) for bus travel to Coventry Airport on 15th August 1976. The event was an Air Display organised by the RAF Association Midland Area. Sadly, the event was cancelled, so presumably the tickets were never actually used. The Adult ticket (Fig 77) was blue, and the Child (Fig 78) pink, with black lettering on both.   (A)

2) Still in Coventry, I have "discovered" (thanks to Mac Cooper) a 2p brown prepaid ticket illustrated in Fig 79. These were produced in sheets of 20, and were based very closely on Coventry City Transport issues. No doubt there were other values, but details are not known. Dating is (I assume) about 1974.   (A)

Page 18   There was also a BCT ½d white token, but this had been withdrawn before WMPTE took over.   (A)

Chronology   The formation date of WMPTE should, of course, read 1 Oct.1969. A ghastly mistake!

Part 3 Travelcards.

No additions or corrections to report.

Although *Parts 1-3* included a large number of illustrations, I became conscious of the fact that certain types of ticket (or related items) had not been adequately illustrated, in some cases because no illustration was available at the time.

In an attempt to remedy this, we end this Appendix with 21 additional illustrations relating to tickets described in *Parts 1-3*. (Figs. 80-100)

Fig 77

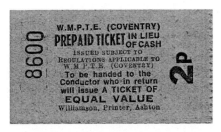

Fig 79

Fig 78

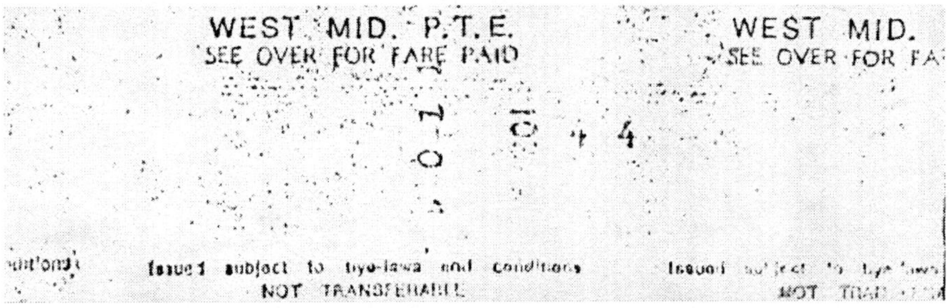

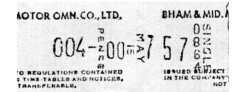

Fig 80
Videmat
Type 1
primrose with red text

Fig 81 - BMMO Setright Type 6

Fig 82 - "Park and Ride" Setright

Fig 83 - Type WM3 roll used in ex-BMMO machine

Fig 84 - Type WM2 roll used by Stevensons, Spath

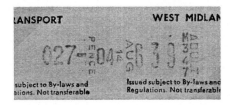

Fig 85 - Type WM4 roll used by Fylde Borough Transport

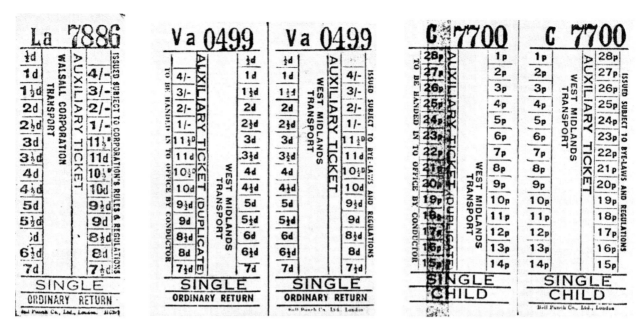

Fig 86 - Walsall
Corporation
Emergency ticket

Figs 87 and 88 - WMPTE (Walsall District) Emergency tickets

Fig 89
Wolverhampton Corporation
TIM machine D

Fig 90
Birmingham CT
TIM machine 1

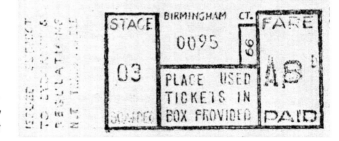

Fig 91
Birmingham CT
TIM machine 66

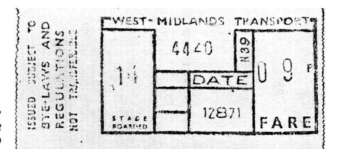

Fig 92
West Midlands PTE Type TIM3
machine N39

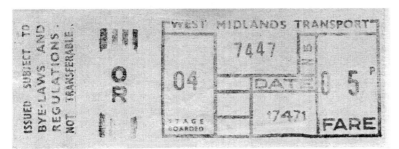

Fig 93
West Midlands PTE Type TIM4
machine N5

Fig 94
West Midlands PTE Type TIM5
machine N101

Fig 95
Mid Warwickshire Motors
Almex 0005

Fig 96
West Bromwich CTD
Almex 0004

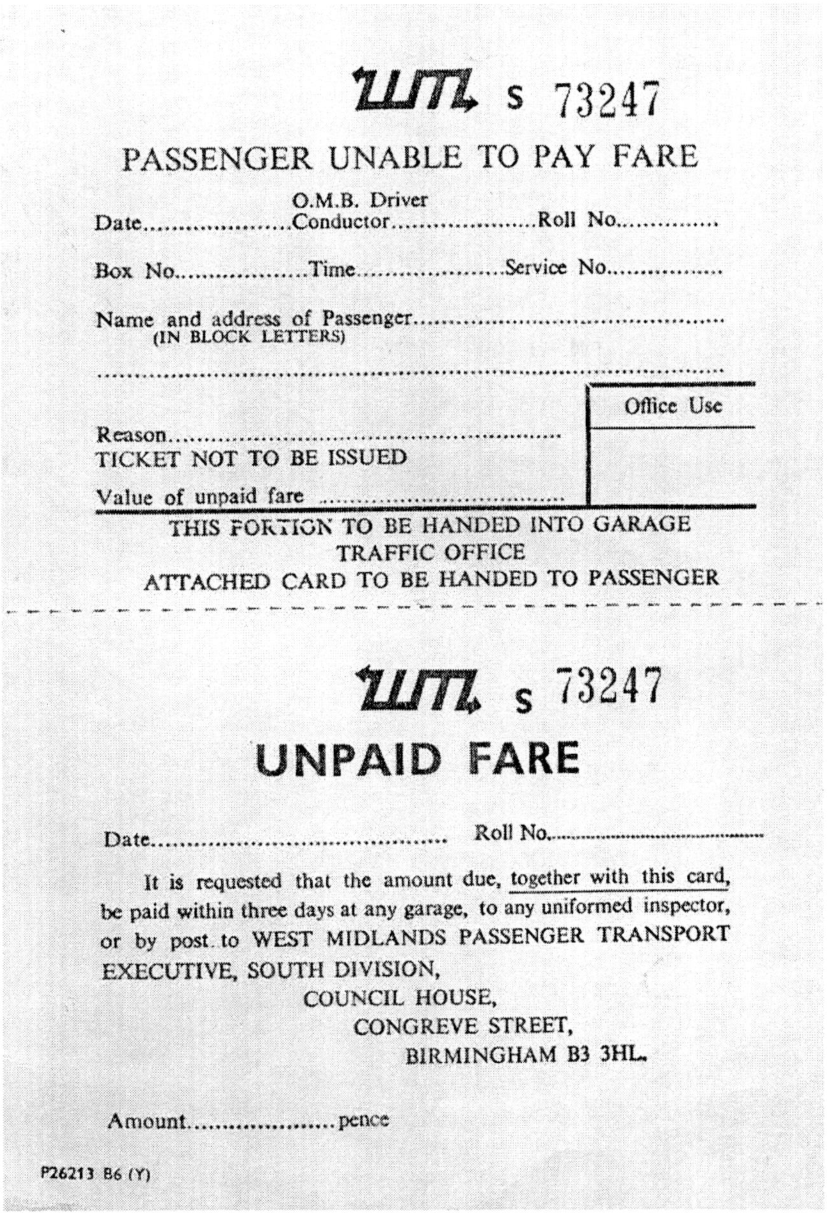

Fig 97
South Division
Unpaid Fare Card

WMT s 73247

PASSENGER UNABLE TO PAY FARE

O.M.B. Driver
Date.....................Conductor.....................Roll No...............

Box No...................Time...................Service No.................

Name and address of Passenger.......................................
(IN BLOCK LETTERS)

....

	Office Use
Reason..	
TICKET NOT TO BE ISSUED	
Value of unpaid fare	

THIS PORTION TO BE HANDED INTO GARAGE
TRAFFIC OFFICE
ATTACHED CARD TO BE HANDED TO PASSENGER

- -

WMT s 73247

UNPAID FARE

Date.............................. Roll No.............................

It is requested that the amount due, together with this card,
be paid within three days at any garage, to any uniformed inspector,
or by post to WEST MIDLANDS PASSENGER TRANSPORT
EXECUTIVE, SOUTH DIVISION,
COUNCIL HOUSE,
CONGREVE STREET,
BIRMINGHAM B3 3HL.

Amount...................pence

P26213 B6 (Y)

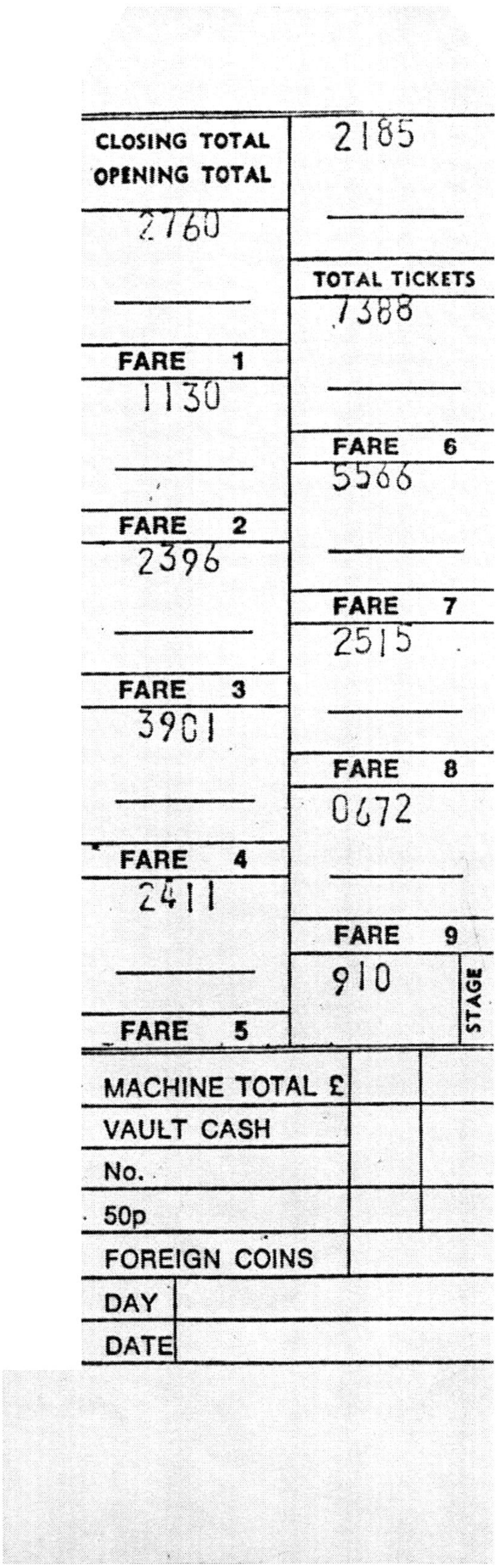

CLOSING TOTAL 2185
OPENING TOTAL 2760

TOTAL TICKETS 7388

FARE 1 1130

FARE 6 5566

FARE 2 2396

FARE 7 2515

FARE 3 3901

FARE 8 0672

FARE 4 2411

FARE 9 910

STAGE

FARE 5

MACHINE TOTAL £
VAULT CASH
No.
50p
FOREIGN COINS
DAY
DATE

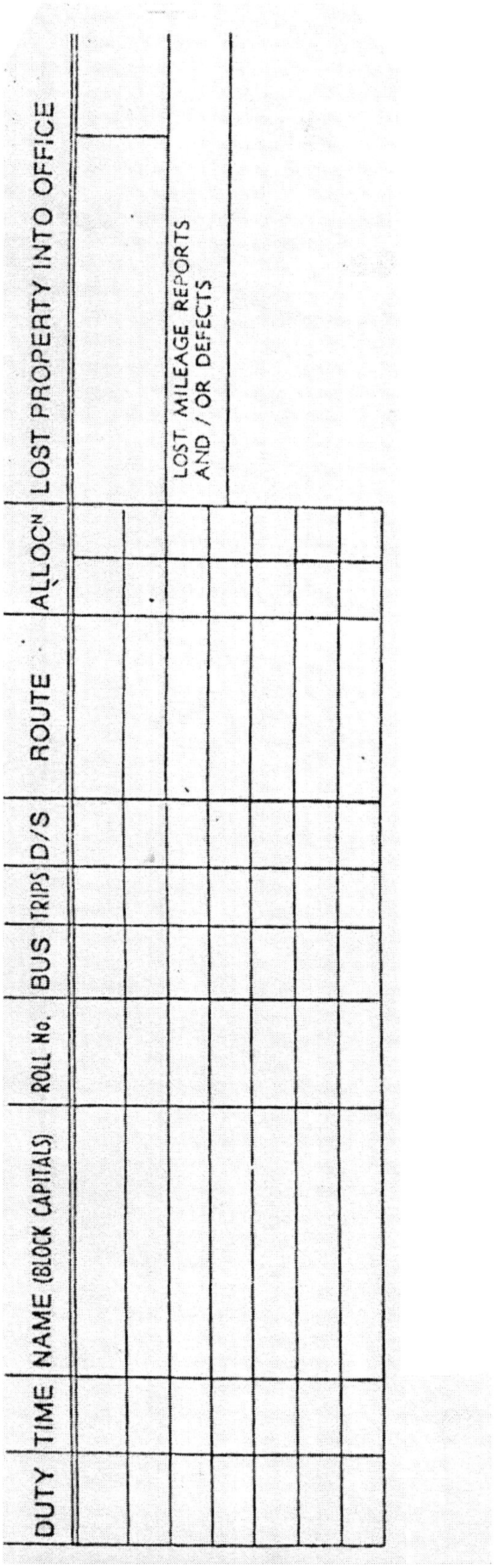

LOST PROPERTY INTO OFFICE
LOST MILEAGE REPORTS AND / OR DEFECTS
ALLOCN
ROUTE
D/S
TRIPS
BUS
ROLL No.
NAME (BLOCK CAPITALS)
TIME
DUTY

Figs 98 and 99 - Sabloc Farestat waybill

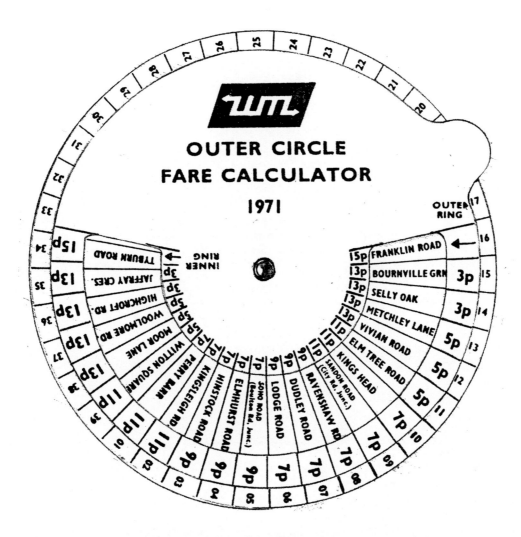

Fig 100 - Plastic fare calculator used by conductors on Birmingham's Outer Circle route.

And last, but not least ....

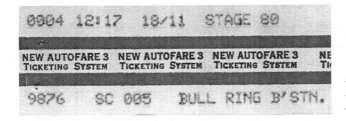

Fig. 101
Demonstration
Autofare 3

Not mentioned previously, this demonstration Autofare 3 ticket dates from around 1982. The printed terminal point, Bull Ring Bus Station, Birmingham, (now closed) is clear evidence that it was used for test purposes by WMPTE, but as far as I know, tickets of this design were never issued to passengers. The preprinted text was black with two broad, red, continuous bands.

Other Publications

Tickets of the West Midlands PTE - Robin Oliver

Part 1 - Machine-issued Tickets	**£2.00**
Part 2 - Miscellaneous Tickets	**£1.50**
Part 3 - Travelcards	**£2.50**

London Transport Numerical Stage Punch Tickets - Bob Williamson

Checklists of all known "deaf and dumb" type punch tickets from 1933 onwards.

Part 1 - Tram and Trolleybus	**£3.50**
Part 2 - Central Buses	**£3.50**
Part 3 - Country Buses and Green Line Coaches	**£2.50**
Part 4 - Prepaids	**£3.50**
Part 5 - Miscellaneous	**£3.50**

London in 1997 - Brian Pask

Comprehensive survey of tickets and ticket systems in the Capital, covering bus, tube, rail and river services.   **£2.50**

INTIS - Brian Boddy

The British Rail Intermediate Ticket Issuing System: a comprehensive guide in two volumes. (*)   **£8.00**

Greater Manchester in 1998/9 - Paul J Smith and Brian Hughes

Complete survey of tickets and ticket systems, covering bus, tram and rail. (*)   **£4.50**

The Tickets of the Grimsby & Immingham Electric Railway - Brian Pask

All known tickets described, with numerous illustrations, faretables and map. (*)   **£4.75**

The Tickets of Hants & Dorset Motor Services 1920-1987 - Part 1 - Punch Tickets - Andrew Waller

Exhaustive history detailing all known punch tickets. Fully-illustrated with tickets, faretables and two maps. (*)   **£5.50**

South Yorkshire Supertram - Fares and Ticketing - 1994-1997 - Dave Aspinwall

A compilation of tables and diagrams, detailing fares, tickets and machine validations. Fully illustrated. (*)   **£5.50**

* including illustrations in colour

All prices include postage and packing. Order from the Publication Sales Officer:

Steve Skeavington [X]
6 Breckbank,
Forest Town,
Mansfield,
NG19 0PZ

The Transport Ticket Society

..... offers something for everyone interested in the study and collection of transport tickets, whether casual collector or serious student:

- Monthly, illustrated *Journal* with ticket news from the UK and around the world, articles on tickets, both historical and present-day, and much more.
- Regular distributions of obsolete transport tickets from the UK and overseas.
- Ticket exchange pools, circuits and postal auctions.
- Publications on tickets and related topics.
- Extensive library of ticket and transport items.
- Regular meetings in London, Manchester and Birmingham.

For a *FREE* sample Journal and membership details, send two first-class stamps to the Membership Secretary:

Courtney Haydon [X]
4 Gladridge Close
Earley, Reading
RG6 7DL

E-Mail: courtney@gladridgecl.demon.co.uk

http://www.btinternet.com/~transport.ticket